A Syllabus of Japanese Civilization

by H. Paul Varley

Second Edition

Columbia University Press
New York & London
1972

Portions of this work were prepared under a contract with the U.S. Office of Education for the production of texts to be used in undergraduate education. The texts so produced have been used in the Columbia College Oriental Humanities program and have subsequently been revised and expanded for publication in the present form. Copyright is claimed only in those portions of the work not submitted in fulfillment of the contract with the U.S. Office of Education. The U.S. Office of Education is not the author, owner, publisher, or proprietor of this publication, and is not to be understood as approving by virtue of its support any of the statements made or views expressed therein.

Copyright © 1968, © 1972 Columbia University Press
ISBN 0-231-03677-9
Printed in the United States of America

FOREWORD

This syllabus is one of a series of aids to the study of Asian civilizations prepared under the auspices of the University Committee on Oriental Studies for use in introductory courses and as a reference for general readers. It is meant to serve as a guide to essential information, bibliography, and questions of general interpretation, not as a cram book or as a substitute for reading and discussion.

Preparation of this syllabus was undertaken at the suggestion of a conference on undergraduate foreign area studies held at the Office of Education, Washington, D.C. in November of 1964. The original draft was prepared with the support of that office, and on the basis of experience in use has been revised to produce the present version. No doubt further revisions will be undertaken from time to time. To that end comments and suggestions are invited by the editors. It should be recognized, however, that a good syllabus always excludes more than it includes.

Wm. Theodore de Bary

INTRODUCTION

Since a syllabus is, by its very nature, highly selective, any attempt on my part to anticipate or to ward off criticism in these introductory pages would be both futile and improper. Indeed it is my sincere hope that those who use this outline and its appended materials will use them critically. I shall limit myself here to general comments on my approach to their compilation and to suggestions on how they may be used.

Periodization. Traditional Japan, from around the fifth until the seventeenth century A.D., lends itself conveniently to a chronological breakdown. The Tokugawa period (1600–1867) and the modern era, on the other hand, seem to be best approached from a more topical standpoint. I cannot, however, defend the precise arrangement of topics which I have adopted other than to say that it has worked smoothly for me in classroom presentation.

Subject Matter. Each teacher and student will wish to stress different aspects of Japanese civilization. I have attempted to summarize the major political, social, religious, intellectual, economic, and artistic developments in Japan from earliest times to the present. It seems hardly necessary to observe that some understanding of the broad outlines of Chinese civilization is virtually mandatory for the student of Japanese affairs. Coverage of religious and intellectual trends in particular must presuppose a basic knowledge of the Buddhist and Confucian traditions before they were introduced to Japan.

Names and Dates. The selection of names and dates for inclusion in a syllabus of this nature is extremely difficult. Some facts are of such importance that they could scarcely be omitted. Others have been entered solely in the hope that they are more significant or more representative than comparable ones that have been left out. I do think it unlikely that the teacher of an introductory course on Japan will want his students to commit to memory all the names and dates contained here. The teacher must determine the quota of these facts most appropriate to his particular course.

Reading Assignments. It is strongly recommended that *Sources of Japanese Tradition* be used as a basic text for students in any course on Japanese civilization. In the premodern section of such a course the teacher might appropriately assign as supplementary classroom reading either *East Asia: The Great Tradition* or *Japan: A Short Cultural History* and, if there is time to deal more fully with the literary tradition, the Keene *Anthology*. For modern Japan, I would suggest that *Sources of Japanese Tradition* be used with any one of the other four texts listed.

Additional Readings. This is a selected list for teachers and others who wish to go more deeply into the various aspects of Japanese civilization. Since there is very little material in English on certain periods and topics of premodern Japan, selection has sometimes been governed entirely by what is available. On other periods, especially the modern, it has been necessary to choose from among various readings according to certain guidelines. Books have been favored over journal articles and, where possible and appropriate, newer books have been preferred to older and probably less accessible ones. Some excellent, but highly specialized, studies have been omitted because I have deemed them too detailed or too complex for introductory purposes. For additional information on bibliography the best work to consult is Bernard S. Silberman, *Japan and Korea: A Critical Bibliography,* Tucson: The University of Arizona Press, 1962. Materials published since 1962 may be found in the September (Bibliography) issues of the *Journal of Asian Studies.* Finally, teachers are strongly urged to read the bibliographic essay by John W. Hall entitled *Japanese History: New Dimensions of Approach and Understanding* (Service Center for Teachers of History publication no. 34), Washington, D.C.: Service Center for Teachers of History, American Historical Association, 1961.

Discussion Topics and Questions. It is hoped that these topics and questions will be useful to the teacher both in his preparation of lectures and in his initiation of class discussion on the major themes of Japanese civilization.

Abbreviations of texts in the Reading Assignments sections need no special explanation. For readings from *Sources of Japanese Tradition,* I have given page numbers for both the hardbound and the two-volume paperback edition.

Proper names are rendered in the Japanese order of family name followed by given name.

I should like to thank my colleagues at Columbia University who have read this syllabus and have commented on it: Professors Wm. T. de Bary, Mason Gentzler, Donald Keene, James Morley, Ivan Morris, Marleigh Ryan, Arthur Tiedemann, and Herschel Webb. It is usual at times such as this, having acknowledged help received from others, to absolve them immediately of any and all responsibility for errors that still remain in the text. In the case of this syllabus it is absolutely necessary to make clear that I alone am responsible for its basic form and general topical arrangement. The readers mentioned above, short of suggesting that I start over again, could scarcely do more than advise me on specific points. For such advice I am most grateful.

H. Paul Varley

Columbia University
May, 1968

CONTENTS

TRADITIONAL JAPAN   1

MODERN JAPAN   43

MAPS   I. Famous Cities and Places in Japanese History   86
        II. Mito and the Great Western *Han* of the Late Tokugawa Period   86
        III. The Japanese Empire Before World War II   88

PRONUNCIATION GUIDE   91

GLOSSARY OF TERMS   93

GUIDE TO ILLUSTRATIVE MATERIALS   97

Traditional Japan

BOOKS FOR ASSIGNED READINGS

Books on Traditional Japan
Keene, Donald (ed.). *Anthology of Japanese Literature From the Earliest Era to the Mid-Nineteenth Century*. New York: Grove Press, 1955. Paperback, 1960. Selected translations, with brief introductory comments, from the masterworks of traditional Japanese literature.
Reischauer, Edwin O., and John K. Fairbank. *East Asia: The Great Tradition*. Boston: Houghton Mifflin, 1960. The first of two volumes of *A History of East Asian Civilization*. The section on Japan is a well-balanced treatment of nearly all phases of Japanese civilization up to the nineteenth century.
Sansom, G. B. *Japan: A Short Cultural History*. Revised edition. New York: Appleton-Century-Crofts, 1962. First written in 1931, this work has not been superseded as the best English language source for the major themes of Japanese cultural history through the first half of the nineteenth century. Political events are, for the most part, covered only in summary.
Tsunoda, Ryusaku, Wm. Theodore de Bary, and Donald Keene. *Sources of Japanese Tradition*. New York: Columbia University Press, 1958. Paperback (in two volumes), 1964. A source book on Japanese intellectual history with valuable commentaries and interpretive essays. The first half, on traditional Japan, is concerned mainly with Shinto, Buddhism, and Confucianism. For antecedent material on Buddhism and Confucianism, see the companion works of this series: *Sources of Indian Tradition* and *Sources of Chinese Tradition*.

Other Recommended General Readings
Anesaki Masaharu. *History of Japanese Religion*. London: Kegan Paul, Trench, Trubner, 1930. The work of a prominent prewar Japanese scholar.

Brower, Robert H., and Earl Miner. *Japanese Court Poetry.* Stanford: Stanford University Press, 1961. This is not an easy book for those who, without knowledge of the Japanese language, are just beginning the study of Japan. But it must be noted here as a work of first importance on the technical analysis and appreciation of the kinds of poetry produced by Japan's court aristocracy from earliest times until the mid-fourteenth century.

Eliot, Sir Charles N. E. *Japanese Buddhism.* Second edition. New York: Barnes and Noble, 1959. Long a standard study of the historical development of Japanese Buddhism.

Hall, John W. *Japan, from Prehistory to Modern Times.* New York: Delacorte, 1970. Paperback, 1971. This is a sound and analytical treatment of Japan's past, although the stress is overwhelmingly on institutional history. Also, the coverage is far more abundant for the premodern period than the modern.

Keene, Donald. *Japanese Literature: An Introduction for Western Readers.* New York: Grove Press, 1955. A short, expertly written book on various aspects of Japanese literature, including poetry, the theatre, and the novel.

Miller, Roy Andrew. *The Japanese Language.* Chicago: University of Chicago Press, 1967. A detailed and comprehensive description of the history and structure of the Japanese language.

Munsterberg, Hugo. *The Arts of Japan: An Illustrated History.* Rutland, Vermont, and Tokyo: Tuttle, 1957. Paperback, 1962. An introduction, with excellent accompanying photographs, to the major themes and masterpieces of the visual arts in Japanese history: painting, sculpture, architecture, pottery, etc.

Noma Seiroku. *The Arts of Japan, Ancient and Medieval.* Translated and adapted by John Rosenfield. Tokyo: Kodansha, 1965. This is an impressively illustrated book on Japanese art up to the sixteenth century. The author discusses the great works of visual art during this period by grouping them according to their locales—Nara, Kyoto, Kamakura, etc.

Paine, Robert T., and Alexander Soper. *The Art and Architecture of Japan.* Baltimore: Penguin Books, 1955. Contains much information about Japanese art and architecture in the premodern period. The beginner, however, would be well advised to read first the less detailed and more narrative Munsterberg book cited above.

Sansom, George. *A History of Japan to 1334.* Stanford: Stanford University Press, 1958. Paperback, 1969. The first volume of a three-volume series on the premodern period by this century's most distinguished Western scholar of Japan. The coverage, with emphasis on political and social developments, is detailed and the style is of the highest literary quality.

Sansom, George. *A History of Japan, 1334–1615*. Stanford: Stanford University Press, 1961. Paperback, 1969. A colorful treatment of the long-neglected medieval centuries of Japanese history with intimate glimpses into the lives of courtiers and warriors through their diaries and personal records. Marred only by an excessive attention to the military campaigns which accompanied the dynastic struggles of the fourteenth century.

Sansom, George. *A History of Japan, 1615–1867*. Stanford: Stanford University Press, 1963. Paperback, 1969.

Tokyo National Museum (comp.). *Pageant of Japanese Art*. Six volumes. Tokyo: Toto Bunka, 1952–54. By far the most comprehensive survey of Japanese art available in English. It covers the following fields: volumes I and II, painting; volume III, sculpture; volume IV, ceramics and metalwork; volume V, lacquer art and textiles; volume VI, architecture and gardens. The illustrative plates are excellent.

I. GEOGRAPHIC SETTING
   A. Four major islands: Honshu, Kyushu, Shikoku, Hokkaido
   B. Temperate climate and abundant rainfall
   C. Insularity: approximately 115 miles from Korean peninsula
   D. Great alluvial plains: Kantō (eastern provinces), Kinai or Kansai (home provinces), Nōbi (region of Nagoya); growth as great population centers
   E. Mountainous nature of land: approximately 15–17 per cent arable land

Reading Assignments
Reischauer and Fairbank, *The Great Tradition,* 450–56.

Additional Readings
Ginsberg, Norton (ed.). *The Pattern of Asia.* Englewood Cliffs, New Jersey: Prentice-Hall, 1958. Chapter 3 deals with the East Asian setting, 46–59.
Hall, John W., and Richard K. Beardsley. *Twelve Doors to Japan.* New York: McGraw-Hill, 1965. Essays on various aspects of Japanese culture and society. Chapter 1 is entitled "A Geographic Profile of Japan." See especially 2–18.
Sansom, George, *A History of Japan to 1334.* See Chapter 1, "The Land," 3–11.
Trewartha, Glenn T. *Japan: Physical, Cultural and Regional Geography.* Madison: University of Wisconsin Press, 1945.

Discussion Topics and Questions
1. Significance of geographic isolation in Japanese history.
2. Comparison of influence of geography on historical development of Japan and England.

II. SHINTO AND JAPAN'S MYTHOLOGICAL ORIGINS
  A. Shinto (Way of the Gods), the native faith
    1. Primitive animism and polytheism
    2. Concern with defilement and stress on purification or ritual lustration; taboos, but no true ethical code
    3. Concept of *kami* ("upper" or "superior") : distinction between deities and men not clearly drawn
    4. No central church organization; on the contrary, diversity of cults and many independent local shrines; inseparability of religious authority and social structure
  B. Mythological origins
    1. Creation story; Izanagi and Izanami as progenitors of Japanese islands and numerous deities
    2. Sun Goddess (Amaterasu Ōmikami), central figure in Shinto pantheon
    3. Ninigi's descent to Japan in possession of sacred regalia (mirror, sword, jewel)
    4. Emperor Jimmu, earthly descendant of Sun Goddess
    5. Jimmu's eastward campaign to region of Yamato Plain
    6. Jimmu's rites to Sun Goddess (February 11, 660 B.C.) : traditional date for founding of Japanese Empire

Reading Assignments
Reischauer and Fairbank, *The Great Tradition,* 464–69.
Sansom, *A Short Cultural History,* 22–63.
Sources of Japanese Tradition, 14–35; I, 12–33.

Additional Readings
Chamberlain, Basil H. (tr.). *Kojiki or Records of Ancient Matters.* Second edition. Kobe: J. L. Thompson, 1932. Translation of the oldest Japanese historical records.
Aston, Wm. G. (tr.). *Nihongi: Chronicles of Japan from the Earliest Times to A.D. 697.* Reprint. London: Allen and Unwin, 1956. Translation of another early history of Japan.
Holtom, Daniel C. *The National Faith of Japan.* London: Kegan, Paul, Trench, Trubner, 1938. A rather lengthy treatment of the historical development of Shinto with analogies drawn from the mythologies and religions of other cultures.
Muraoka Tsunetsugu. *Studies in Shinto Thought.* Tokyo: Ministry of Education, 1964. Translation of a series of essays by a noted Japanese scholar. Chapters 1 and 2 deal with the general nature of Shinto and its early development.

Discussion Topics and Questions
1. Episodes in Shinto mythology that seem to be based on actual historical experience.
2. Early Shinto as the mythology of an agrarian people.
3. Supposed foundations of the Japanese imperial line.
4. Shinto mythology and Chinese-style history in legends of *Kojiki* and *Nihon Shoki*.

III. PRE- AND PROTO-HISTORICAL PERIOD
  A. Paleolithic culture (possibly from ca. 500,000 B.C.): chipped stone tools, but no pottery
  B. Jōmon culture (from ca. 8000 B.C.): mesolithic or early neolithic
    1. Hand-made pottery with "rope-pattern" surface decorations; hunting and gathering of roots; fishing, shell mounds; sunken-pit dwellings
    2. Located largely in north and east
  C. Yayoi culture (from ca. 300 B.C.)
    1. Knowledge of bronze and iron; agriculture (wet-rice culture); wheel-made pottery
    2. Typical sites in west and east
  D. Emishi: driven eastward and northward by migration of historic Japanese from west; problem of relationship to proto-caucasian Ainu
  E. Tomb culture (from ca. 300 A.D.): probably extension of Yayoi under new influences from continent
    1. Large stone burial chambers
    2. *Haniwa* figurines as representations of aristocratic, horse-riding people
    3. South seas or "southern" element in Shinto architecture: Ise and Izumo shrines

Reading Assignment
Reischauer and Fairbank, *The Great Tradition*, 456–62.

Additional Readings
Beardsley, Richard K. "Japan Before History," *Far Eastern Quarterly*, XIV, no. 3 (1955), 317–46. A concise survey of more recent trends and interpretations in Japanese archaeology.
Kidder, Jonathan E. *Japan Before Buddhism*. London: Thames and Hudson, 1959. A detailed and abundantly illustrated study of early Japan.
Kidder, Jonathan E. *The Birth of Japanese Art*. London: George Allen and Unwin, 1965. On premodern figurines and related items of plastic art.

IV. EARLIEST WRITTEN RECORDS (FROM CHINESE DYNASTIC HISTORIES)
  A. In *History of Kingdom of Wei* (compiled ca. A.D. 297) : account of land of Wa consisting of 100 communities
  B. In *History of Latter Han Dynasty* (compiled ca. A.D. 445)
    1. Envoy from Wa to Chinese Emperor Kuang-wu (A.D. 57)
    2. Emergence of shamanistic ruler Pimiko (Himiko) at head of Yamatai (Yamato?) : problem of location of Yamatai
  C. In *History of Liu Sung Dynasty* (compiled ca. A.D. 513) : fifth-century requests to China for confirmation of Japanese military overlordship of Korea; pledges of loyalty to Chinese throne

Reading Assignments
Reischauer and Fairbank, *The Great Tradition,* 462–64.
Sources of Japanese Tradition, 3–14; I, 1–12.

Additional Reading
Tsunoda, Ryusaku (ed. and tr.). *Japan in the Chinese Dynastic Histories (later Han through Ming dynasties).* Pasadena: Perkins, 1951.
Young, John. *The Location of Yamatai: A Case Study of Japanese Historiography.* (Johns Hopkins University Studies in History and Political Science, Series 75, No. 2) Baltimore: Johns Hopkins University Press, 1958.

Discussion Topics and Questions
1. Attitudes of Chinese toward Japan during the earliest years of contact.

V. YAMATO PERIOD, OR AGE OF CLANS (ca. 400–645)
A. Emergence of Yamato Clan (ca. 400–552)
1. Social structure
   a. Great clans (*uji*) : located mainly in central provinces; Yamato (Imperial) Clan most important; clan members (*ujibito*) as upper, aristocratic level of society
   b. Occupational groups (*be*) attached to clans: lower, nonaristocratic social strata; largest groups engaged in agriculture, but others devoted to fishing, special crafts, etc.
2. Religious foundations of rule
   a. Clan deities (*ujigami*) : Sun Goddess (deity of preeminent Yamato Clan) as national progenitor
   b. Emperor (head of Yamato Clan) : sacerdotal and political roles
3. Political structure
   a. *Kabane:* titles granted to clan leaders (*uji no kami*)
   b. Great clans as occupational groups for Yamato Court (e.g., Mononobe, or Armorers; Nakatomi, or Court Ritualists)

B. Renewed contact with the continent and Japan's response (552–645)
1. Introduction of Buddhism (552 *) : carrier of continental culture
2. "Progressives" (Soga) versus "conservatives" (Mononobe, Nakatomi) at Court
3. Soga family in power: sponsorship of Buddhism; marital policy toward imperial family
4. Prince Shōtoku (574–622) : prelude to Chinese-style reform
   a. Twelve-cap ranking system (603) : attempt to establish Chinese-style bureaucracy
   b. Seventeen-article constitution (604) : largely Confucian ideals; but also call for reverence of Buddhist treasures
   c. Dispatch of students to Sui China
5. Foreign relations
   a. Decline of Japanese influence in Korea
   b. Unification of China under Sui-T'ang and Korea under Silla; fear of military intervention and movement for reform in Japan

---

* A suggested alternate date is 538.

c. Commencement of official missions to Sui (607) and T'ang (630) China
6. Asuka art: wooden buildings and sculpture of Hōryūji

Reading Assignments
Reischauer and Fairbank, *The Great Tradition*, 469–78.
Sansom, *A Short Cultural History*, 64–81.
Sources of Japanese Tradition, 36–69; I, 34–67.

Additional Readings
Hall, John W. *Government and Local Power in Japan, 500 to 1700*. Princeton: Princeton University Press, 1966. A specialized study of the province of Bizen, but also valuable for an understanding of general sociopolitical developments. See 3–44 for introduction to Japanese institutional history and for Yamato period.

Discussion Topics and Questions
1. The Emperor as a political and religious or sacerdotal leader.
2. The importance of familial relations in early Japanese society; birth as the main qualification for social advancement.
3. Buddhism as the principal carrier of continental culture to Japan.
4. Prince Shōtoku's Seventeen Articles as a "constitution"; as a synthesis of foreign philosophies and native attitudes.

VI. TAIKA REFORM, 645–710: INFLUENCE OF CHINESE INSTITUTIONS
  A. Destruction of Soga in palace coup (645)
  B. Stages of reform
    1. Land redistribution and regional administration
      a. Equal-field system
      b. Threefold tax: harvest; special products; corvée and miscellaneous labor (including military conscription)
      c. Division of country into provinces (*kuni*), districts (*gun*), and townships (*ri*)
    2. Establishment of central administrative structure and adoption of legal provisions: Taihō Code (701)
      a. Central structure: Department of Rites; Department of State (Chancellor; Ministers of Left and Right; Eight Ministries)
      b. Legal provisions: *ritsu* (penal); *ryō* (administrative)
    3. Founding of permanent capital at Nara (710): modeled on T'ang capital of Ch'ang-an; minting of coins and improved transportation to meet new urban demands
  C. Continuing compromises with great clans: appointment of clan heads as district officials; allowances on land
  D. Elimination of Japanese influence in Korea (663)
  E. Emergence of Fujiwara as foremost ministerial family at Court: Nakatomi Kamatari granted name Fujiwara by Emperor Tenji (r. 668–71)
  F. Jinshin Incident (672): rise to power of Emperor Temmu (r. 673–86) and consolidation of Taika land reform

Reading Assignments
Reischauer and Fairbank, *The Great Tradition,* 478–79.
Sansom, *A Short Cultural History,* 82–106.
Sources of Japanese Tradition, 70–92; I, 68–90.

Additional Readings
Asakawa, K. *The Early Institutional Life of Japan: A Study in the Reform of 645 A.D.* Second edition. New York: Paragon Book Reprint Corp., 1963. Reprint of a pioneer work, first published in 1903, on the Taika Reform by a distinguished Japanese scholar.
Hall, *Government and Local Power in Japan, 500 to 1700.* A modern, interpretive approach to the Taika Reform, 45–65.
Sansom, George B. "Early Japanese Law and Administration." *Transactions of the Asiatic Society of Japan,* 2d series, X (1932),

67–110; XI (1934), 117–50. Translation of and detailed notes on the administrative and legal codes adopted at this time and modified during the next few centuries.

Discussion Topics and Questions
1. Attitudes of Japanese leaders toward China: to what extent were they selective in their adoption of Chinese methods of government and social control?
2. To what extent was the T'ang land system appropriate and readily adaptable to seventh-century Japan?
3. In what ways was the Taihō Code a culmination of the ideals of Prince Shōtoku?
4. Was the Taika Reform a revolution?

VII. NARA PERIOD, 710–794
  A. Writing of history and poetry
    1. *Kojiki* (Records of ancient matters, 712); *Nihon Shoki* (Chronicles of Japan, 720), first of Six National Histories
    2. Anthologies
      a. *Man'yōshū:* poems of native freshness and vigor; evolution of predominant *waka* form of poetry
      b. *Kaifūsō:* Chinese-style poems
  B. Atypical social and political mobility based on qualifications other than birth: Chinese learning and Buddhist priesthood
  C. Buddhism
    1. Six Nara sects (Sanron, Jōjitsu, Kusha, Hossō, Ritsu, Kegon): abstruse doctrines and limited followings
    2. Sutra of the Golden Light
    3. Building of great temples at Nara
    4. Attempt to use Buddhism as institutional and ideological means for strengthening state: Emperor Shōmu (r. 724–49)
      a. Erection of Tōdaiji and Daibutsu (Eastern Great Temple and Great Statue of Buddha)
      b. Construction of provincial branch temples (*kokubunji*) and nunneries
    5. Gyōki (668–749) and small number of "popular priests"
  D. Breakdown of equal-field system and first phase of estate, or manor (*shōen*), formation
    1. Unequal distribution of fields: extra allotments and tax-free status granted to aristocrats and religious institutions
    2. Difficulties of periodic reallotment
    3. Avoidance of tax registers and abandonment of fields; growing number of *rōnin* (socially displaced people)
    4. Absorption of abandoned fields and opening of new lands by aristocrats and religious institutions; private employment of *rōnin*
    5. Inability of central government to control provincial officials
  E. Affair of Empress Kōken (r. 749–58 and, as Shōtoku, 764–70) and the priest Dōkyō (d. 772): climax of tendency on part of Buddhist priests to seek influence and high position at Court

  F. Shōsōin: repository of eighth-century decorative arts
  G. Decision to move from Nara: reaction to empresses, political priests, and this-worldy aspects of Nara Buddhism
  H. Late Nara reforms
    1. Elimination of excess officials
    2. Reduction in corvée labor requirements
  I. Temporary transfer of capital to Nagaoka (784–94)

Reading Assignments
Keene, *Anthology*, 33–60.
Reischauer and Fairbank, *The Great Tradition*, 479–91, 494–98.
Sansom, *A Short Cultural History*, 107–84.
Sources of Japanese Tradition, 93–110; I, 91–108.

Additional Reading
The Manyōshū. New York: Columbia University Press, 1965. Selected translations, originally published in 1940, of poems from the great eighth-century anthology.

Discussion Topics and Questions
1. Importance of Chinese learning during the eighth century.
2. The relationship between Buddhism and state centralization.
3. Impact of Buddhism on native Shinto: what sort of synthesis evolved?
4. What factors were involved in the decision to move from Nara?

HEIAN PERIOD, 794-1185

VIII. EARLY HEIAN PERIOD, 794-967
A. Reign of Emperor Kammu (r. 781-806)
 1. Move of capital to Heian (Kyoto): good outlets by river to sea; accessibility by principal land route (Tōkaidō) to eastern provinces
 2. Campaigns against Emishi: Tamuramaro (758-811) as Barbarian-subduing Generalissimo (*Sei-i Tai-shōgun*)
B. Buddhism: mountain sects
 1. Tendai: Saichō (767-822); temple on Mt. Hiei; importance of Lotus Sutra; eclecticism; monasticism
 2. Shingon (True Word): Kūkai (774-835); temple on Mt. Kōya; esotericism; iconography and art; appeal to Kyoto aristocrats
C. Efforts to adjust Taika-Taihō structure
 1. Military: abandonment of conscription system (792); district officials to be responsible for future recruitment
 2. Provincial administration: assignment of inspectors to deal with improper practices and to ensure flow of tax revenue
 3. Central administration: establishment of offices outside Taihō Code
  a. Sovereign's Private Office (*Kurōdo-dokoro*)
  b. Office of Imperial Police (*Kebiishichō*)
 4. Legal: amendment and clarification of *ritsu-ryō* provisions to meet more closely the needs of a developing Japanese state and society
  a. *Kyaku* (adjustments by decree)
  b. *Shiki* (detailed rules)
D. Last official mission to T'ang China (838): end of direct Chinese influence
E. Struggle for political supremacy between Emperors and Fujiwara family
 1. Fujiwara marital policy toward imperial family
 2. Fujiwara Yoshifusa as Regent (*Sesshō*) for minor Emperor Seiwa (r. 858-76)
 3. Fujiwara Mototsune as Civil Dictator (*Kampaku*) for adult Emperor Kōkō (r. 884-87)
 4. Scholar-minister Sugawara Michizane (845-903) enlisted by Emperor Uda (r. 887-97) in unsuccessful attempt to check Fujiwara

F. "Golden" reign of Emperor Daigo (r. 897–930)
   1. Suspension of Fujiwara regency
   2. Code of Engi: important legal supplement
   3. Completion of last of Six National Histories
   4. Compilation of *Kokinshū* (Collection of ancient and modern poems)

IX. MID-HEIAN PERIOD, OR AGE OF "POWER AND GLORY" OF FUJIWARA REGENTS, 967–1068
   A. Political developments
      1. Monopolization of central offices by Fujiwara
      2. Child Emperors and early abdications: Emperors from Reizei (r. 967–69) through Goreizei (r. 1045–68) virtually powerless
      3. 995–1068: high point of Fujiwara rule under Michinaga (966–1027) and Yorimichi (992–1074)
   B. Cultural and artistic flowering
      1. Evolution of native scripts (*katakana, hiragana*)
      2. Brilliant aristocratic society in capital: thoroughly civilian; rigidly stratified; highly refined and inbred; premium on style and taste
      3. Great literature produced by court ladies in Japanese (Yamato) language
         a. Personal diary (*nikki*): e.g., *The Gossamer Years*
         b. Poem-tale (*uta-monogatari*) : *Tales of Ise*
         c. Novel: Lady Murasaki, *Tale of Genji* and aesthetic principle of *aware*
         d. Miscellany: Sei Shōnagon, *Pillow Book* and aesthetic principle of *okashi*
      4. Yamato-e narrative scrolls: development of a native style of painting
   C. Affairs in the provinces
      1. Second phase of estate formation (see Nara Period for first phase characterized by opening of new lands)
         a. Commendation of fields to aristocrats and religious institutions, especially during tenth century
         b. Continued decrease in public domain and shrinkage of tax revenue of central government
         c. Fujiwara political eminence accompanied by vast increases in family estate holdings
      2. Origins of a military class
         a. Need for self-protection in outlying regions
         b. Search for new opportunity in provinces: by distant members of imperial family (granted names Taira and Minamoto) ; by Fujiwara not belonging to favored branch at capital
         c. Military disturbances from mid-tenth century: revolts

of Taira Masakado 939–40, Fujiwara Sumitomo 941, Taira Tadatsune 1028–31; Former Nine-Years War 1051–62 (based on years of actual fighting), Later Three-Years War 1086–88

d. Appointment of provincial leaders as constabulary officials (from ca. 1000)

X. LATE HEIAN PERIOD, 1068–1185
  A. Emperor Gosanjō (r. 1068–72)
    1. First Emperor since ninth century without Fujiwara mother; age 35 at accession; determined to curb Fujiwara power
    2. Records Office (*Kirokujo*): to assert control over formation and extension of estates
    3. Early abdication to establish office of Cloistered Emperor, but died following year (1073)
  B. Period of challenge to Fujiwara rule by Cloistered Emperors (*In*) (1086–1156)
    1. Avoidance of burden of ritual and ceremony demanded of Emperor
    2. Accumulation of estates for office of Cloistered Emperor
    3. Engagement of non-Fujiwara (e.g., Minamoto) officials
  C. Political instability and strife in the capital (1156–59)
    1. Fujiwara: quarreling among themselves; faced with opposition from other families
    2. Imperial family: disputes between Emperors and Cloistered Emperors
    3. Warring monks: rowdyism
    4. Taira and Minamoto: growing importance as leaders of military class
    5. Struggle for supremacy in the capital in armed conflicts of 1156 and 1159: victory of Taira
  D. Supremacy of Taira (1159–85)
    1. Taira Kiyomori (1118–81): imitated Fujiwara policy toward imperial family; concentrated on affairs in Kyoto and neglected provinces
    2. Trade with Sung China: development of port of Fukuhara (Kobe)
    3. Taira seen as "haughty"; their fall regarded as inevitable
    4. Minamoto regrouping in east
    5. Gempei War (1180–85): victory of Minamoto; exploits of Yoshitsune (1158–89)

Reading Assignments
Keene, *Anthology*, 63–176.
Reischauer and Fairbank, *The Great Tradition*, 491–94, 498–518.
Sansom, *A Short Cultural History*, 185–269.
Sources of Japanese Tradition, 111–84; I, 109–80.

Additional Readings

Heian diaries in translation: Earl Miner (tr.). *Japanese Poetic Diaries*. Berkeley: University of California Press, 1969; Ivan Morris (tr.). *As I Crossed a Bridge of Dreams*. New York: Dial, 1971; Edward G. Seidensticker (tr.). *The Gossamer Years*. Tokyo: Tuttle, 1964.

McCullough, Helen C. (tr.). *Tales of Ise*. Stanford: Stanford University Press, 1968.

Morris, Ivan. *The World of the Shining Prince*. New York: Knopf, 1964. Penguin Paperback, 1969. An eminently readable, scholarly account of court life during the Heian period.

Morris, Ivan (tr.). *The Pillow Book of Sei Shōnagon*. Two volumes. New York: Columbia University Press. 1967. Paperback, 1970. Complete translation (volume I) with copious annotations (volume II) of the noted miscellany of Court society.

Murasaki Shikibu. *The Tale of Genji*. Translated by Arthur Waley. New York: Modern Library, 1960. Translation of the greatest single work in Japanese literature.

Reischauer, Edwin O. *Ennin's Travels in T'ang China*. New York: Ronald Press, 1955. Based on the diary of a prominent Buddhist priest who traveled in China in the mid-ninth century; excellent for a comparison of Chinese and Japanese societies toward the end of Japan's long period of cultural borrowing. An unabridged translation of Ennin's diary may be found in a companion volume, *Ennin's Diary: The Record of a Pilgrimage to China in Search of the Law*.

Discussion Topics and Questions

1. Failure of the Taika land reform and the growth of private estates.
2. From mid-ninth century: the evolution of more indigenous cultural forms and ruling institutions.
3. What is meant by the phrase "rule of taste" as it applies to court society of the Heian period?
4. Compare the society of the Heian capital, as it evolved during the time of Lady Murasaki (ca. 1000), with that of the earlier T'ang capital of Ch'ang-an.
5. What were the bases of Fujiwara power?
6. Why did a military society emerge in the provinces during the later centuries of the Heian period?
7. Reasons why the Taira were unable to establish their rule on a lasting basis.

XI. KAMAKURA PERIOD, 1185–1333: TRANSITION TO MEDIEVAL SOCIETY
   A. Minamoto Yoritomo (1147–99) as Shogun
      1. Aristocratic lineage, charismatic qualities
      2. Authority derived from Emperor
      3. Relationship of loyalty and performance between Shogun and retainers, or housemen (*gokenin*) : importance of landholding and its confirmation
      4. Failure to provide effectively for succession to office of Shogun
   B. Shogunate (*Bakufu*) at Kamakura
      1. Central offices: Board of Retainers; Administrative Board; Board of Inquiry
      2. Regional officials
         a. Constables (*shugo*) : assigned to provinces
         b. Stewards (*jitō*) : appointed to estates
      3. Economic base: landed holdings in east; confiscated Taira estates in west
   C. Problem of Japanese feudalism: applicability of term; comparison with European institutions
   D. Rule of Hōjō Regents: emerged supreme in power struggle among eastern chieftains following Yoritomo's death; appointed Fujiwara and, later, imperial princes as figurehead Shoguns; exercised real authority as Shogunate Regents (*Shikken*)
      1. Unsuccessful attempt by Cloistered Emperor Gotoba (1180–1239) to destroy Hōjō (Jōkyū Incident, 1221)
      2. Hōjō Yasutoki (Regent, 1224–42)
         a. Council of State (*Hyōjōshū*, 1225)
         b. Jōei Code (1232)
      3. Efficiency of Hōjō judicio-legislative practice: settlement of land claims
   E. Kamakura Buddhism
      1. Background factors: decline of Kyoto aristocracy and rise of provincial warriors; time of warfare and natural disasters; pessimism and sense of crisis over "end of the Buddhist law" (*mappō*) ; restricted appeal of complex esoteric practices
      2. Popular sects: offshoots from Tendai synthesis
         a. Pure Land (Jōdo) Buddhism: Hōnen (1133–1212) ; faith in saving grace of Amida Buddha and efficacy of

nembutsu (invocation of Buddha): promise of paradise after death
   b. True (Shin) Sect of Pure Land Buddhism: Shinran (1173–1262); further simplification of Amidist practice; direct appeal to peasant class; abandonment of priestly celibacy
   c. Nichiren Buddhism: dominant personality of founder, Nichiren (1222–82); primacy of Lotus Sutra; militancy and intolerance; Japan-centeredness
  3. Zen (Meditation) Buddhism: appeal to the intuitive; stress on art and aesthetics
   a. Rinzai Sect: Eisai (1141–1215); importance of *kōan*
   b. Sōtō Sect: Dōgen (1200–53) and stress on *zazen* (sitting in meditation)
F. Kamakura art
  1. Continuation of Yamato-e: more detailed and realistic style; scrolls depicting warfare and lives of famous Buddhist priests
  2. Sculpture: Unkei and the "Nara Renaissance"; great statue of Buddha at Kamakura
G. Literary developments
  1. Continuation of aristocratic tradition: Fujiwara Teika (1162–1241) and *Shinkokinshū* (New *Kokinshū*)
  2. Transition from aristocratic refinement to more realistic style: *Hōjōki* (An account of my hut)
  3. New genre of war-tales: *Tale of the Heike*
H. Mongol invasions: unsuccessful attempts in 1274 and 1281; "divine winds" (*kamikaze*)
I. Post-invasion years and decline of the Shogunate
  1. Continuing disintegration of estate system
  2. Weakening of ties between Kamakura and regional officials
  3. Commercial development and growth of money economy; alienation of houseman lands; issuance of debt-cancellation decrees (*tokusei*)
  4. Cost to Shogunate of maintaining defense against Mongol threat; inability to satisfy demands for reward
  5. Decrease in quality and exercise of Hōjō leadership
  6. Dynastic dispute within imperial family: junior and senior lines

Reading Assignments
Keene, *Anthology*, 179–228.
Reischauer and Fairbank, *The Great Tradition*, 519–52.
Sansom, *A Short Cultural History*, 270–347.
Sources of Japanese Tradition, 185–256; I, 181–250.

Additional Readings
Anesaki, Masaharu. *Nichiren, The Buddhist Prophet.* Cambridge: Harvard University Press, 1916. This is a dated and overly sentimentalized study, but it is still useful for information on Nichiren's life and beliefs.
Asakawa, Kan'ichi. *Land and Society in Medieval Japan.* Tokyo: Japan Society for the Promotion of Science, 1965. This collection of Asakawa's writings includes the articles "The Life of a Monastic *Shō* in Medieval Japan" (1916) and "Some Aspects of Japanese Feudal Institutions" (1918). Although quite dated, Asakawa's work is still important to the student of early Japanese land and feudal institutions.
Bloom, Alfred. *Shinran's Gospel of Pure Grace.* Tucson: University of Arizona Press, 1965. A concise treatment of the thought of the great thirteenth-century founder of the True Sect of Pure Land Buddhism.
Dumolin, Heinrich. *A History of Zen Buddhism.* New York: Random House, 1963. McGraw-Hill Paperback, 1965. One of the best single volumes on Zen Buddhism. Chapter 10 on Dōgen, 151–74, is especially excellent.
Duus, Peter. *Feudalism in Japan.* New York: Knopf Paperback, 1969. A short, but useful, introduction to the subject of Japanese feudalism.
Hall, John W. "Feudalism in Japan: A Reassessment," in Hall and Marius B. Jansen (eds.). *Studies in the Institutional History of Early Modern Japan.* Princeton: Princeton University Press, 1968. Paperback, 1970. Pp. 15–51. One of the most important attempts to define the term "Japanese feudalism" and to test its usefulness in the study of comparative institutions.
Sadler, Arthur L. (tr.). "Heike Monogatari," *Transactions of the Asiatic Society of Japan*, 1st series, XLVI (1918), 1–278; XLIX (1921), 1–354. Translation of one of the earliest and, literarily, the most admired of the medieval war tales.
Shinoda, Minoru. *The Founding of the Kamakura Shogunate, 1180–*

1185. New York: Columbia University Press, 1960. The expository portion, 3–144, serves as an excellent introduction to the formation of military society and the founding of Japan's first warrior government. Appended is a partial translation of *Azuma Kagami*, an important record of Shogunate affairs during the Kamakura period.

Reischauer, Edwin O. "Japanese Feudalism" in Rushton Coulburn (ed.), *Feudalism in History*. Princeton: Princeton University Press, 1956. A brief discussion of the feudal process in Japan from the twelfth through the nineteenth centuries, 26–48.

Varley, H. Paul. *Samurai*. New York: Delacorte, 1971. Dell Paperback, 1972. A brief survey of the history of Japan's premodern warrior class.

Warner, Langdon. *The Enduring Art of Japan*. Cambridge: Harvard University Press, 1952. Grove Press (Evergreen) Paperback, 1958. A collection of impressions, written in a lively style, of Japan's artistic tradition. Pp. 47–52 contain an especially lovely description of the distinctive Japanese scroll paintings of the Kamakura period.

Discussion Topics and Questions
1. What was the attitude of Minamoto Yoritomo toward the Imperial Court?
2. The development of feudal institutions.
3. Reasons for the spread of popular Buddhist sects.
4. Why did Zen Buddhism appeal to the medieval warrior? How widespread was its appeal?
5. Nichiren and the Mongol invasions: a growing sense of "nationalism" in Japan.
6. The practice of meditation in the Buddhist tradition.

KEMMU RESTORATION AND MUROMACHI PERIOD

XII. KEMMU RESTORATION, 1333-1336

A. Victory of supporters of Emperor Godaigo (r. 1318-39) of junior line over Hōjō; exemplary behavior and military prowess of Kusunoki Masashige (d. 1336), later to be regarded as greatest of Imperial Loyalists

B. Anachronistic attempt to return to "golden" period of Emperor Daigo and to exercise "direct" imperial rule

C. Estrangement of Ashikaga Takauji (1305-58) and flight of Godaigo to Yoshino

Additional Readings

Varley, H. Paul. *Imperial Restoration in Medieval Japan.* New York: Columbia University Press, 1971. An examination of the institutional and intellectual backgrounds of the Restoration, and a study of the imperial succession dispute as a problem in Japanese historiography.

XIII. EARLY ASHIKAGA, OR MUROMACHI, PERIOD, 1336–1477
A. War between the Courts (1336–92)
 1. Northern Court (senior line) at Kyoto, backed by Ashikaga
 2. Southern Court (junior line) at Yoshino
B. Ashikaga Shogunate
 1. Founded at Kyoto
 2. Retention of major offices of Kamakura Shogunate
C. Rule of Ashikaga Yoshimitsu (Shogun 1368–94, d. 1408)
 1. Balance of power between Shogunate and constable-daimyos
 2. Unification of Northern and Southern Courts (1392)
 3. Problem of Japanese pirates (*wakō*) ; trade with Ming China
D. Decline of Ashikaga Shogunate
 1. Succession disputes within constable-daimyo families
 2. Dispute over successor to Yoshimasa (Shogun 1443–72)
 3. Ōnin War (1467–77) : devastation of Kyoto
E. Economic and commercial developments
 1. Agriculture: opening of new fields; cooperative irrigation; improved tools; extensive use of fertilizers; widespread double-cropping
 2. Commerce: growth of towns and markets; craft and commodity guilds (*za*) ; circulation of Chinese copper coins; transportation, storage, and wholesale functions
F. Muromachi culture
 1. Determinants
   a. Merging of courtier and warrior societies in Kyoto
   b. Influence of Zen and Zen priests
 2. Period of Yoshimitsu: Kinkakuji (Temple of the Golden Pavilion) ; literature and scholarship of leading Zen temples; *Nō* theatre (Zeami, 1363–1443 or 1445)
 3. Period of Yoshimasa: Ginkakuji (Temple of the Silver Pavilion) ; tea ceremony; monochrome painting (Shūbun; Sesshū, 1420–1506) ; landscape gardening
 4. Literature
   a. Linked verse (*renga*)
   b. Continuation of miscellany tradition: *Tsurezuregusa* (Essays in idleness) of Kenkō (1282–1350)

G. Religion: renewed interest in Shinto from time of War Between the Courts; Kitabatake Chikafusa (1293–1354) and the question of imperial legitimacy in *Jinnō Shōtōki* (Record of direct descent of divine sovereigns)

XIV. LATE MUROMACHI, OR PROVINCIAL WARS, PERIOD, 1477–1573
  A. Conditions following Ōnin War: *gekokujō* (those below overthrow those above); spread of fighting to provinces; failure of central control; decline of constable-daimyos; peasant uprisings
  B. Growth of new daimyo class: independence of Shogunate; autonomous domains; development of strong soldieries; building of castle towns; encouragement of agriculture and commerce; house laws
  C. Foreign contacts
    1. Arrival of Portuguese (1543); trade and Christian missionary activity; founding of Nagasaki (1570)
    2. High point of piracy in 1550s

Reading Assignments
Keene, *Anthology*, 231–331.
Reischauer and Fairbank, *The Great Tradition*, 552–78.
Sansom, *A Short Cultural History*, 348–400.
Sources of Japanese Tradition, 256–303; I, 250–97.

Additional Readings
Dumoulin, *A History of Zen Buddhism*. Chapter II, "The Cultural Influence of Zen in the Muromachi Period," 175–97.
Hall, John W. "Foundations of the Modern Japanese Daimyo," in Hall and Jansen (eds.), *Studies in the Institutional History of Early Modern Japan*, 65–77. An analysis of the development of the daimyo during the medieval and Tokugawa periods.
Hall, John W. "The Castle Town and Japan's Modern Urbanization," in Hall and Jansen (eds.), *Studies in the Institutional History of Early Modern Japan*, 167–88. Interpretive article on the important process of urbanization in the medieval and Tokugawa periods.
Keene, Donald (tr.). *Essays in Idleness: The Tsurezuregusa of Kenkō*. New York: Columbia University Press, 1967.
Keene, Donald. *Nō, the Classical Theatre of Japan*. Tokyo: Kodansha, 1966. A large and magnificently illustrated book dealing with the various aspects of *nō* and *kyōgen*: their history, their texts as literature, performances, etc.
Keene, Donald (ed.). *20 Plays of the Nō Theatre*. New York: Columbia University Press. 1970. Paperback, 1970.

McCullough, Helen C. (tr.). *The Taiheiki*. New York: Columbia University Press, 1959. Translation of the first third of a lengthy war tale dealing with the fourteenth-century dynastic split.

Varley, H. Paul. *The Ōnin War*. New York: Columbia University Press, 1967. Contains a survey of the institutional aspects of military history in Japan from the thirteenth through the mid-fifteenth century and a selective translation of the *Chronicle of Ōnin*.

Wang I-t'ung. *Official Relations Between China and Japan, 1368–1549*. Cambridge: Harvard University Press, 1953. A scholarly treatment of Japan's limited foreign relations and trade during most of the Muromachi period.

Discussion Topics and Questions

1. The ideal of "restoration" in Japanese history.
2. Trade with Ming China: why did the Chinese desire a renewal of relations?
3. What were the origins of the Ōnin War?
4. Zen Buddhism and Muromachi aesthetics. The aesthetic principles of *yūgen, miyabi,* and *sabi* in terms of continuity from a courtier- to a warrior-dominated culture.
5. The art of Sesshū: his indebtedness to Chinese masters; his originality and place within the native tradition.

XV. PERIOD OF UNIFICATION, 1573–1600
A. Ideal of unification in Japanese history
B. Oda Nobunaga (1534–82)
 1. Early stages of unification: entry into Kyoto (1568); removal of last Ashikaga Shogun (1573)
 2. Castle town at Azuchi; encouragement of commerce
 3. Campaigns against Buddhist temples: burning of temple on Mt. Hiei (1571); occupation of Ishiyama Castle in Osaka (1580)
 4. Assassination of Nobunaga
C. Toyotomi Hideyoshi (1536–98)
 1. Completion of unification
 2. Castle town at Osaka; interest in commercial cities
 3. Establishment of a national land policy and a fixed social order
   a. Land surveys
   b. Separation of farmer and warrior, of rural and urban classes
 4. Overseas trade: desire for additional revenue; competition with Western nations
 5. Korean invasions (1592 and 1597): unsuccessful attempts to expand militarily on continent
 6. Belated effort to provide for succession of son Hideyori (1593–1615)
D. Momoyama art: building of great castles and palaces; screen paintings; Namban (Southern Barbarian) pictures; ceramic and lacquer wares; textiles
E. Tokugawa Ieyasu (1542–1616): victory in Battle of Sekigahara (1600); appointed Shogun (1603); destruction of Toyotomi family at siege of Osaka Castle (1615)

Reading Assignments
Reischauer and Fairbank, *The Great Tradition,* 579–90.
Sansom, *A Short Cultural History,* 401–40.
Sources of Japanese Tradition, 305–31; I, 298–322.

Additional Readings
Boxer, Charles R. *The Christian Century in Japan.* Berkeley: University of California Press, 1951. The standard work on the first phase of Western contact with Japan.
Cooper, Michael. *They Came to Japan.* Berkeley: University of California Press, 1965. An annotated collection of eye-witness

accounts of foreigners in Japan, 1543–1640. Contains fascinating details of Japanese life and customs during the heroic age of unification.

Hall and Jansen (eds.), *Studies in the Institutional History of Early Modern Japan.* A collection of articles—some new, some previously published in journals—on developments in law, daimyo rule, local administration, urbanization, etc., during the late medieval and "early modern" (i.e., Tokugawa) periods.

Kondo Ichitaro. *Japanese Genre Painting: The Lively Art of Renaissance Japan.* Translated by Roy Andrew Miller. Rutland, Vermont, and Tokyo: Tuttle, 1961.

Kuno Yoshisaburo. *Japanese Expansion on the Asiatic Continent.* Two volumes. Berkeley: University of California Press, 1937–40. This work, although dated, contains much information on Japanese relations with the Asian mainland since earliest times. Chapter 4 in volume I, 129–78, deals with Hideyoshi's invasions of Korea. Primary source documents are appended.

Discussion Topics and Questions

1. Unification: what institutional developments on the local and regional levels made it possible? What degree of unification was actually attained?

2. What lasting impact, if any, did Christianity and Western culture have on Japan during the sixteenth and early seventeenth centuries?

XVI. ESTABLISHMENT OF TOKUGAWA, OR EDO, SHOGUNATE

A. Tokugawa Shogunate
   1. Central organization: Shogun; Council of Elders (*Rōjū*); Junior Elders (*Wakadoshiyori*); Chamberlains (*Soba-yōnin*); Inspectors (*Metsuke*); Commissioners (*Bugyō*)
   2. Economic base
      a. Control of approximately 25 per cent of rice-producing land in country
      b. Supervision of politically and commercially important cities, mines, etc. (e.g., Kyoto, Osaka, Nagasaki, Sado)
B. Daimyos and their domains (*han*)
   1. Types of daimyos: *shimpan* (collateral); *fudai* (hereditary); *tozama* (outside)
   2. Shogunate control of daimyos: shifting of domains, system of alternate attendance in Edo; extraordinary levies; laws for the military houses
   3. Domainal administration: gathering of retainers in castle towns; establishment of offices similar to Shogunate; collection of rice tribute from peasantry
C. Trade, Christianity, and the seclusion policy
   1. Arrival of Dutch and British (ca. 1600)
   2. Demand for Chinese silk: triangular trade with European nations
   3. Growing fear of Christianity: persecutions; Shimabara Revolt (1637)
   4. Seclusion edict (1639): foreign contacts to be restricted to Dutch and Chinese at Nagasaki
D. Social ordering: warrior, farmer, artisan, merchant

Assigned Readings
Reischauer and Fairbank, *The Great Tradition*, 590–613.
Sansom, *A Short Cultural History*, 441–70.
Sources of Japanese Tradition, 331–43; I, 322–34.

Additional Readings
Boxer, *The Christian Century in Japan*. See the portions dealing with the seclusion policy.
Hall, John W. *Tanuma Okitsugu (1719–1788): Forerunner of Modern Japan*. Cambridge: Harvard University Press, 1955. This

work, cited elsewhere for its main topic, contains an excellent introductory section, 21-33, on the Tokugawa administrative system.

Hall, *Government and Local Power in Japan, 500 to 1700.* Chapter 12, "The Establishment of the Tokugawa Hegemony," 330-74, is the best and most detailed source in English on the steps taken by the Tokugawa to assert their control over Japan in the early seventeenth century.

Totman, Conrad D. *Politics in the Tokugawa Bakufu, 1600-1843.* Cambridge: Harvard University Press, 1967. Topically organized description of the military, administrative, and economic aspects of the government of the Tokugawa Shoguns. Gives particular attention to the relations between the Shoguns and their vassals.

Discussion Topics and Questions

1. Appropriateness of the term "centralized feudalism" as applied to the Tokugawa state.
2. Seclusion policy: reasons for implementing it; its effects on Japanese historical development.

XVII. TOKUGAWA PERIOD: ECONOMIC AND CULTURAL DEVELOPMENTS

A. Economic and commercial advancements: vast increase in agricultural productivity during first century; spread of money economy; urbanization (e.g., Edo, Osaka, Kyoto); expansion of wholesale facilities; water transportation

B. Intellectual trends
  1. Neo-Confucianism
     a. Role of Zen priests in introducing Confucian teachings to Japan: Fujiwara Seika (1561-1619)
     b. Orthodox (Chu Hsi) school: rationalism, historicism, humanism, anti-commercialism, ethnocentrism, isolationism
        1) Hayashi Razan (1583-1657) and state sponsorship
        2) Historical writing of the Mito School: *Dai Nihon Shi* (History of great Japan)
     c. Ōyōmei (Wang Yang-ming) school: intuition-in action
        1) Nakae Tōju (1608-48) : life of withdrawal
        2) Kumazawa Banzan (1619-91) : political career programs for reform
  2. School of Ancient (Confucian) Studies
     a. Yamaga Sokō (1622-85) : way of the warrior (*bu shidō*)
     b. Itō Jinsai (1627-1705) : Confucian scholarship; humanistic ideals
     c. Ogyū Sorai (1666-1728)
  3. Mid-Tokugawa rationalism: Arai Hakuseki (1657-1725), Shogunate adviser and scholar
  4. Shinto revival (School of National Learning)
     a. Rejection of Confucian ethics; search for a canonical literature
     b. Motoori Norinaga (1730-1801) : study of *Kojiki* reaction to rationalism and stress on emotional side of human nature
  5. Dutch studies: research into practical Western subject

C. Genroku (1688-1703) culture: primarily an urban, merchant phenomenon
  1. Novel: Saikaku (1642-93)
  2. Puppet theatre: Chikamatsu (1653-1724)

3. *Kabuki:* influence of puppet theatre on its themes and acting styles
4. Poetry: Bashō (1644–94) and the perfection of *haiku*
D. Painting: most important development in *ukiyo-e* (pictures of the floating world) depicting chiefly scenes and people of urban pleasure quarters, landscapes

Assigned Readings

Keene, *Anthology,* 335–415.
Reischauer and Fairbank, *The Great Tradition,* 614–19, 626–68.
Sansom, *A Short Cultural History,* 471–513.
Sources of Japanese Tradition, 344–551; I, 335 and *passim* II, 46.

Additional Readings

Bellah, Robert N. *Tokugawa Religion.* Glencoe, Illinois: Free Press, 1957. A highly interpretive work, of major importance, dealing with the "early modern" values and attitudes of the Tokugawa Japanese.

Boxer, Charles R. *Jan Campagnie in Japan, 1600–1850.* Second revised edition. The Hague: Martinus Nijhoff, 1950. A scholarly narrative of the Dutch settlement at Nagasaki and its influence on the small group of Japanese scholars concerned with Western studies.

Ernst, Earle. *The Kabuki Theatre.* New York: Oxford University Press, 1956. Grove Press Paperback. A thorough study of *kabuki:* background, plays, performance, etc. Well illustrated.

Henderson, Harold G. *An Introduction to Haiku.* New York: Doubleday, 1958. Paperback. This is a brief, charmingly written book on the composition and pleasures of *haiku.* Contained are many selections from Bashō, Buson, Issa, Shiki, and others.

Hibbett, Howard S. *The Floating World in Japanese Fiction.* New York: Oxford University Press, 1959. Grove Press Paperback, 1960. Study of Genroku culture with selected translations from Ejima Kiseki and Ihara Saikaku.

Ihara Saikaku. *The Life of an Amorous Woman and Other Writings.* Edited and translated by Ivan Morris. New York: New Directions, 1963. Paperback, 1969. In addition to translations, abundantly annotated, of some of Saikaku's most important works, there are an extensive introduction and several valuable appendices on sources, money, and the hierarchy of courtesans during the Genroku period.

Keene, Donald. *Bunraku: The Art of the Japanese Puppet Theatre.* Tokyo: Kodansha, 1965. Text with detailed and especially excellent photographs of the puppets, their operators, settings, etc.

Keene, Donald (tr.). *Major Plays of Chikamatsu.* New York: Columbia University Press, 1961. Paperback, 1964. Introduction, appendices, and translations of eleven of Chikamatsu's works.

Keene, Donald. *The Japanese Discovery of Europe: Honda Toshiaki and Other Discoverers, 1720–1798.* London: Kegan Paul, 1952. Stanford Paperback (revised), 1969. A most readable survey of Dutch studies and Japanese contacts with Europeans during the Tokugawa period; with selected translations of the writings of Honda Toshiaki.

McEwan, J. R. *The Political Writings of Ogyū Sorai.* Cambridge, England: Cambridge University Press, 1962. A concise book of translations, with commentary, of the political statements of a prominent mid-Tokugawa period Confucian adviser to the Shogunate.

Michener, James A. *The Floating World.* New York: Random House, 1954. A popular narrative of the history and development of woodblock prints with a good selection of prints appended.

Sheldon, Charles D. *The Rise of the Merchant Class in Tokugawa Japan, 1600–1868: An Introductory Survey.* Locust Valley, N.Y.: J. J. Augustin, 1958.

Smith, Thomas C. *The Agrarian Origins of Modern Japan.* Stanford: Stanford University Press, 1959. Athenium Paperback, 1966. An important work, based on Japanese research, on the Tokugawa farming village.

Discussion Topics and Questions

1. Urbanization and the development of commerce: Tokugawa Japan as an early modern state.
2. Why was Sung Neo-Confucianism especially appropriate as an orthodox creed for the Tokugawa state?
3. Neo-Shinto: its relationship to other systems in the Japanese tradition that stress the intuitive rather than the rational.
4. Importance of urban pleasure quarters in a society that sought to minimize romantic love.
5. The development of a modern, scientific attitude among scholars of Dutch studies.

XVIII. DECLINE AND DESTRUCTION OF THE TOKUGAWA SYSTEM
  A. Discontent within the system
    1. Takenouchi Shikibu (1712–67) and Yamagata Daini (1725–67) : criticism of military government and plea for return to imperial rule
    2. Social disequilibrium: prosperity of merchants; economic difficulties within farming and warrior classes
  B. Efforts to reinvigorate the system
    1. Reforms of Yoshimune (Shogun, 1716–45) : call for frugality and military spirit; financial retrenchment; land reclamation and diversification of crops; legal revisions
    2. Kansei (1789–1800) reforms of Matsudaira Sadanobu (1758–1829) : reaction to policies of Shogunate Chamberlain Tanuma Okitsugu (in power 1764–86) ; ban on heterodox studies; anticommercial measures
    3. Tempō (1830–43) reforms of Mizuno Tadakuni (1793–1851) : modeled on earlier reforms
  C. Western intrusion
    1. Accidental foreign contacts: e.g., shipwrecks
    2. Intentional violations of Japanese exclusion policy
      a. Russian explorers and traders from the north
      b. British warship "Phaeton" at Nagasaki (1808)
      c. United States mercy ship "Morrison" at Uraga (1837)
      d. Arrival of Commodore Matthew Perry (1853) and Treaty of Friendship with United States (1854)
    3. Vacillation of the Shogunate
      a. 1806 decision to extend courtesies to accidental intruders but to maintain basic exclusion policy
      b. 1825 decree calling for immediate repulsion of foreigners ("Don't Think Twice" edict)
      c. 1842 return to earlier policy of polite but firm attitude toward foreign intrusion
  D. Debate over the Tokugawa system: reappraisal of relationship between Emperor and Shogun; call for renewal of national spirit and strengthening of defenses; problem of foreign relations and of reopening country (to what extent? at what time?) ; demand for broadening of participation in national affairs

1. Mito School
   a. *Sonnō-jōi* (revere the Emperor! expel the barbarians!)
   b. Tokugawa Nariaki (1800–60): opposition to entrenched *fudai* bureaucracy and call for views of great *tozama* daimyos
2. Sakuma Shōzan (1811–64)
   a. *Kaikoku* (open the country) policy
   b. Eastern morals and western technology
   c. Proposal for union of Court and Shogunate
3. Yoshida Shōin (1830–59) and anti-Shogunate activism
E. Forces potentially destructive of the Tokugawa system
   1. Foreign powers: military threat
   2. Great western *han:* Satsuma, Chōshū, Tosa, Hizen
   3. "Enlightened" samurai: informed criticism; desire to participate in central affairs
   4. Imperial Court: rallying point for loyalist sympathizers and the disaffected
   5. Peasant unrest
F. Expansion of foreign contacts and final years of the Tokugawa Shogunate (Bakumatsu period, 1853–67)
   1. Townsend Harris and a commercial treaty with the United States: beginning of unequal treaties based on extraterritoriality, import duty restrictions, and most-favored-nation provisions
   2. Ii Naosuke (1815–60) as Great Elder (*Tairō*), 1858–60: attempt to protect position of entrenched *fudai* bureaucracy through reimposition of firm Shogunate rule and purges
   3. 1860–66: rapprochement between Shogunate and great *tozama* daimyos: but growing anti-Shogunate sentiment among samurai and other loyalist groups
      a. Military campaigns against Chōshū: defeat of Shogunate army during second campaign (1866) by joint Satsuma-Chōshū force
      b. Abolition of Shogunate (1867)

Assigned Readings
Reischauer and Fairbank, *The Great Tradition,* 619–26.
Fairbank, Reischauer, and Craig, *The Modern Transformation,* 179–225.

Sansom, *A Short Cultural History*, 513–24.
Sources of Japanese Tradition, 552–622; II, 47–115.

Additional Readings

Beasley, Wm. G. *Selected Documents on Japanese Foreign Policy, 1853–1868*. London: Oxford University Press, 1955. The introductory section, 1–93, is a tightly written analysis of ideas and events from the arrival of Perry to the Meiji Restoration.

Craig, Albert M. *Chōshū in the Meiji Restoration*. Cambridge: Harvard University Press, 1961. Not only a carefully written study of one of the main *tozama* han, but also a source for analysis and interpretation of a variety of institutional and intellectual developments during the Tokugawa period.

Dore, R. P. *Education in Tokugawa Japan*. Berkeley: University of California Press, 1965.

Earl, David M. *Emperor and Nation in Japan*. Seattle: University of Washington Press, 1964. Part Two, 107–210, deals with the life and thought of Yoshida Shōin.

Hall, *Tanuma Okitsugu (1719–1788): Forerunner of Modern Japan*. Monograph of a chamberlain who exercised great power within the Shogunate, 1764–86.

Harootunian, H. D. *Toward Restoration*. Berkeley: University of California Press, 1970. This is a highly analytical and provocative study of socio-political thought leading to the Meiji Restoration. However, criticism must be made of the paucity of annotations and the absence of a bibliography.

Harris, Townsend. *The Complete Journal of Townsend Harris, First American Consul and Minister to Japan*. Revised edition edited by Mario E. Cosenza. Rutland, Vermont, and Tokyo: Tuttle, 1959.

Jansen, Marius B. (ed.). *Changing Japanese Attitudes Toward Modernization*. Princeton: Princeton University Press, 1965. Paperback, 1969. A collection of essays by some of the most important contemporary Western and Japanese scholars of Japan. For the Tokugawa period see: R. P. Dore, "The Legacy of Tokugawa Education"; Albert Craig, "Science and Confucianism in Tokugawa Japan"; Herschel Webb, "The Development of an Orthodox Attitude toward the Imperial Institution in the Nineteenth Century."

Jansen, Marius B. *Sakamoto Ryōma and the Meiji Restoration*. Princeton: Princeton University Press, 1961. Stanford Paperback,

1971. The story of a Tosa activist during the momentous years leading to the Meiji Restoration.

Sakata Yoshio and John W. Hall. "The Motivation of Political Leadership in the Meiji Restoration," *Journal of Asian Studies,* XVI, no. 1 (1956), 31–50. An important article on approaches to the study of causation in the Meiji Restoration and on political leadership at various stages in the restoration process from 1830 to 1873.

Webb, Herschel. *The Japanese Imperial Institution in the Tokugawa Period.* New York: Columbia University Press, 1968. An examination of the function of the office of Emperor in the Tokugawa period and, in the larger sense, an important contribution to the study of political thought in premodern Japan.

Discussion Topics and Questions
1. The nature of orthodox reform during the Tokugawa period.
2. "Eastern morals and Western technology": is such a proposal a meaningful guideline to modernization?
3. Role of the Western Powers in ending Japanese seclusion.

Modern Japan

BOOKS FOR ASSIGNED READINGS

Books on Modern Japan

Beasley, W. G. *The Modern History of Japan.* New York: Praeger, 1963. Paperback, 1967. Carefully written, with stress on the political, social, and economic, rather than the cultural or intellectual, aspects of Japan's modern history.

Crowley, James B. (ed.). *Modern East Asia: Essays in Interpretation.* New York: Harcourt, Brace & World Paperback, 1970. Outstanding collection of periodized essays on early modern and modern China and Japan by leading scholars. Could well be adapted as a textbook for courses dealing with the more recent past of East Asia.

Fairbank, John K., Edwin O. Reischauer, and Albert M. Craig. *East Asia: The Modern Transformation.* Boston: Houghton Mifflin, 1965. The best single book on modern East Asia. Contains a highly sophisticated, well-balanced, and analytical treatment of modern Japanese history.

Michael, Franz H., and George E. Taylor. *The Far East in the Modern World.* Revised edition. New York: Holt, Rinehart and Winston, 1964. The section on Japan in this text is much shorter than the Japan sections in the Beasley and Fairbank *et al.* works cited above. Probably most useful for a brief introduction to modern Japan, especially when Japan is studied in conjunction with China and the other countries of East Asia.

Tsunoda, Ryusaku, Wm. Theodore de Bary, and Donald Keene. *Sources of Japanese Tradition.* New York: Columbia University Press, 1958. Paperback (in two volumes), 1964. The emphasis in the second half of this work, which deals with modern Japan, is on political and social thought.

Other Recommended General Readings

Benedict, Ruth F. *The Chrysanthemum and the Sword: Patterns of Japanese Culture.* Boston: Houghton Mifflin, 1946. Tuttle Paperback, 1954. A classic study of Japanese attitudes and values written during World War II by an eminent anthropologist whose work had not previously been related to Japan.

Borton, Hugh. *Japan's Modern Century.* New York: Ronald Press, 1970. Revised and updated edition of a detailed study with good balance in the coverage of domestic developments and foreign affairs. Recommended for upper-level college and graduate courses on modern Japan.

Reischauer, Edwin O. *The United States and Japan.* Revised edition. Cambridge: Harvard University Press, 1957. Compass Books Paperback, 1963. An excellent survey, topically written, of Japan in the modern period, its problems and its prospects.

Ward, Robert E., and Dankwart A. Rustow. *Political Modernization in Japan and Turkey.* Princeton: Princeton University Press, 1964. Contains a series of essays, written by specialists, on various aspects of Japan's modernizing process from the Meiji Restoration to the present.

Yanaga, Chitoshi. *Japan Since Perry.* New York: McGraw-Hill, 1949. A veritable compendium of information on modern Japan through the early postwar years. Excellent for reference purposes.

I. MEIJI RESTORATION
   A. Establishment of Imperial Government
      1. Accession of Meiji Emperor (1867)
      2. Promulgation of Charter Oath (1868): commitment to modernization
      3. Transfer of capital to Tokyo
      4. Return of *han* registers (1869): abolition of feudal domains
      5. Adoption of land tax (1873) as basis for modern fiscal policy.
   B. Structure of government and locus of leadership during early Restoration period
      1. Experimentation in traditional and Western forms of government: reinstitution (1871) of eighth-century ruling structure based on Taihō Code; unsuccessful attempt to infuse principle of separation of executive, legislative, and judicial powers
      2. First phase in formation of Meiji ruling oligarchy: tendency for real power to be exercised by small group of Court nobles and samurai
         a. Court nobles: Iwakura Tomomi (1825–83); Sanjō Sanetomi (1837–91)
         b. Samurai: Ōkubo Toshimichi (1830–78, Satsuma); Saigō Takamori (1827–77, Satsuma); Kido Kōin (1833–77, Chōshū); Ōkuma Shigenobu (1838–1922, Hizen)
      3. Completion of Meiji oligarchy during 1880s: restricted to members of Satsuma and Chōshū *han* cliques (*hambatsu*)
   C. Abolition of Tokugawa class system and founding of modern army
      1. Conversion to new society (1871): aristocrats; gentry; commoners
      2. Commutation of samurai stipends (1873–76)
      3. Formation of conscript army: military study mission to Europe (1870); universal conscription law (1873); formation of army general staff (1878); leadership of Yamagata Aritomo (1838–1922, Chōshū)

Reading Assignments
Beasley, *Modern History*, 98–116.
Fairbank, Reischauer, and Craig, *The Modern Transformation*, 225–43.

Michael and Taylor, *Far East in the Modern World*, 236–45.
Sources of Japanese Tradition, 638–54; II, 131–47.

Additional Readings

Hall, John W., "A Monarch for Modern Japan" in Robert E. Ward (ed.), *Political Development in Modern Japan*. Princeton: Princeton University Press, 1968. An important interpretational article on the role of the Emperor as "sacred legitimizer" in the transition from traditional to modern Japan. Pp. 11–64.

Ike, Nobutaka. *The Beginnings of Political Democracy in Japan.* Baltimore: Johns Hopkins Press, 1950. Part One, 3–43, covers the background of the Restoration, the impact of Western political thought and early experimentation with assemblies and constitutions. The remainder of the book deals with the party movement through the promulgation of the Meiji Constitution in 1889.

Jansen, *Changing Japanese Attitudes Toward Modernization*. John W. Hall, "Changing Conceptions of the Modernization of Japan," 7–41; Marius B. Jansen, "Changing Japanese Attitudes Toward Modernization," 43–89.

Norman, E. Herbert. *Japan's Emergence as a Modern State*. New York: Institute of Pacific Relations, 1940. This study is based on prewar Marxian attitudes toward the Meiji Restoration. Some of its interpretations—e.g., that the Restoration was the work of a "feudal-merchant coalition"—have been rejected or revised by more recent scholars. It remains, however, one of the most important interpretive works in English on the early stages of Japan's modernization. See 3–103. Other sections deal with "Early Industrialization," "The Agrarian Settlement and Its Social Consequences," and "Parties and Politics."

Sansom, G. B. *The Western World and Japan*. New York: Knopf, 1958. A study of Japan from the late sixteenth through the nineteenth century with an extensive section on the background history of European contacts with the countries of East Asia. Chapter 13 covers the politcal aspects of the Restoration up to the promulgation of the Meiji Constitution.

Discussion Topics and Questions

1. Was anything "restored" by the Meiji Restoration? Or was it a "revolution"—politically? socially?
2. How did the new ruling clique of the Restoration differ in background, attitudes, etc. from the members of the Council of

Elders who directed Shogunate affairs in the late Tokugawa period?
3. Significance of the slogan "enrich the country, strengthen its arms" as a reflection of emergent nationalistic sentiments.
4. Advantages that Japan possessed at the outset of the Restoration that contributed to her rapid modernization.

II. FOREIGN RELATIONS IN EARLY MEIJI PERIOD
   A. Establishment of Foreign Office (1869) and normalization of relations with major countries
   B. Overriding issue of treaty revision: incentive to modernize and "civilize" country to meet Western standards
   C. Iwakura Mission to United States and Europe (1871–73)
   D. Jurisdictional questions
      1. With China over Korea
         a. Unsuccessful attempts to open normal diplomatic relations with Korea
         b. Debate over plans to invade Korea (1873): defeat of leaders advocating invasion and their withdrawal from oligarchic ruling circles
         c. Commercial Treaty of Kanghwa (1876): opening of Korean ports
         d. Tientsin (Li-Itō) Convention (1885): Sino-Japanese agreement for joint removal of troops from Korea
      2. With China over Ryukyus: Japanese expedition to Formosa (1874) on behalf of massacred Ryukyuan natives; agreement by China to pay indemnity and tacit acknowledgement of Japanese sovereignty over Ryukyus; establishment of Okinawa Prefecture (1879)
      3. With Russia over Sakhalin and Kuriles: treaty (1875) assigning Sakhalin to Russia and Kuriles to Japan

Reading Assignments

Fairbank, Reischauer, and Craig, *The Modern Transformation,* 375–78.

Michael and Taylor, *Far East in the Modern World:* see Reading Assignments for VII.

Sources of Japanese Tradition, 654–62; II, 147–55.

Additional Readings

Conroy, Francis Hilary. *The Japanese Seizure of Korea, 1868–1910.* Philadelphia: University of Pennsylvania Press, 1960. An examination of Japanese-Korean relations from the time of the Meiji Restoration until Japan's annexation of Korea in 1910. See Chapter 1, "Seikan Ron: Insult, Revenge and a Long Shadow," 17–77.

Harrison, John A. *Japan's Northern Frontier.* Gainesville: University of Florida Press, 1953. Study of the Japanese colonization of Hokkaido with special reference to the domestic issues involved.

Jansen, Marius B., "Modernization and Foreign Policy in Meiji Japan" in Ward (ed.), *Political Development in Modern Japan*. On the evolution of a modern diplomacy and a new role in international affairs. Pp. 149–88.

Lensen, George A. *The Russian Push Toward Japan*. Princeton: Princeton University Press, 1959. An important source for Russo-Japanese relations through the early Meiji period.

Discussion Topics and Questions
1. Issues behind the Korean crisis, 1873.
2. Convergence of Russian and Japanese interests in northeast Asia.
3. Impact of the Iwakura Mission on the thinking of Japan's new leaders.

III. OPPOSITION TO MEIJI OLIGARCHY
   A. Armed rebellion
      1. Saga Rebellion (1874)
      2. Satsuma Rebellion (1877)
   B. Demand for representative government
      1. Memorial for popular assembly (1874): criticism of monopoly of power by predominantly Satsuma-Chōshū ministers; beginning of debate over broadening of participation in government
      2. Itagaki Taisuke (1837–1919, Tosa) and early efforts at party organization: restrictive policies of government in regard to freedoms of press, assembly, speech, etc.
      3. Hokkaido colonization scandal; promise of national assembly (1881, to be convened 1890)
      4. Political parties; strong tendency for personalities to be more important than issues or ideologies in the party movement
         a. Liberal Party (Jiyūtō) of Itagaki: influence of ideals of French Revolution (e.g., Rousseau and natural rights democracy), yet still highly "feudal" content to role as opposition group to Meiji oligarchy; support of rural landlord class
         b. Reform Party (Kaishintō) of Ōkuma Shigenobu: Ōkuma's commitment to British-style political gradualism (e.g., J. S. Mill and utilitarianism); representation of urban commercial interests

Reading Assignments
Beasley, *Modern History*, 117–26.
Fairbank, Reischauer, and Craig, *The Modern Transformation*, 278–90.
Michael and Taylor, *Far East in the Modern World*, 245–49.
Sources of Japanese Tradition: see Reading Assignments for VI.

Additional Readings
Akita, George. *Foundations of Constitutional Government in Modern Japan, 1868–1900.* Cambridge: Harvard University Press, 1967. This is a revisionist book aimed at clarifying the process by which constitutional government was instituted in Meiji Japan. Of particular interest is the author's contention that the oligarchs conceived of and evolved constitutionalism on their terms and

according to their time-schedule; that the party movement of the 1870s and 1880s had little, if any, effect on the process leading to promulgation of the Constitution of 1889 and the opening of the first Diet in 1890.

Pittau, Joseph. *Political Thought in Early Meiji Japan, 1868–1889.* Cambridge: Harvard University Press, 1967. This is an authoritative study of the intellectual milieu within which Western constitutional ideas were studied, debated, and at least partly adopted in the Meiji period. The author examines the manner in which the Meiji leaders sought to synthesize their potentially antithetical commitments to authoritarianism and constitutionalism.

Scalapino, Robert A. *Democracy and the Party Movement in Prewar Japan.* Berkeley and Los Angeles: University of California Press, 1953. By far the most important and ambitious attempt by a Western scholar to analyze the political behavior of the Japanese in the modern period. Chapters 2–4 deal with the emergence of the party movement, its philosophic and popular bases, and the events leading to constitutional government.

Discussion Topics and Questions
1. Obstacles to the inauguration of party government.
2. To what extent did the early party advocates sincerely subscribe to the concepts of Western liberalism?
3. Factionalism or cliqueism in Japanese social and political behavior.
4. Relationship of liberalism to nationalism.

IV. EARLY MODERNIZATION AND INDUSTRIALIZATION
  A. First phase: government planning and monopolization of industry (1868–80)
    1. Employment of foreign advisers and adoption of foreign techniques
    2. Heavy taxation of agriculture and favoring of industrial sector of economy
    3. Priority for foreign exports over domestic consumption
  B. Second phase: sale of government industries and withdrawal of government from direct participation in industry (from 1880)
    1. Financial retrenchment, establishment of a modern banking system, and increase of taxes under Matsukata Masayoshi (1835–1924, Satsuma)
    2. Growth of financial combines (*zaibatsu*)
    3. Production of trade staples for acquisition of foreign exchange: cotton and silk textiles
    4. Development of shipping industry
  C. Third phase: maturation of modern industrial complex by World War I

Reading Assignments
Beasley, *Modern History*, 141–51.
Fairbank, Reischauer, and Craig, *The Modern Transformation*, 244–61.
Michael and Taylor, *Far East in the Modern World*, 263–75.

Additional Readings
Allen, G. C. *A Short Economic History of Modern Japan, 1867–1937.* Second revised edition. London: George Allen & Unwin, 1963. Probably the best short study of the subject available.
Hall and Beardsley, *Twelve Doors to Japan.* John W. Hall, "Aspects of Japanese Economic Development," 538–86. A readable and informative essay, by a historian, on Japanese economic developments during the past century. Suggests revisions in the traditional periodization of modern economic growth.
Lockwood, William W. *The Economic Development of Japan; Growth and Structural Change, 1868–1938.* Princeton: Princeton University Press, 1954. Paperback (expanded), 1970.
Lockwood, William W. (ed.). *The State and Economic Enterprise in Japan.* Princeton: Princeton University Press, 1965. Paperback, 1969. A collection of essays by experts on the economic modern-

ization of Japan. Part One deals with the background and Part Two with "The Transition to Industrial Society."

Smith, Thomas C. *Political Change and Industrial Development in Japan: Government Enterprise, 1868–1880.* Stanford: Stanford University Press, 1955. Contains an especially excellent discussion on the sale of government enterprises in the early 1880s.

Discussion Topics and Questions
1. The role of agriculture in Japan's modernization.
2. Japan's experience in industrial modernization as a model for other aspiring non-Western countries.
3. How crucial was the role of the Meiji oligarchy in providing elitist leadership during Japan's early industrial phase?
4. The role of the state and of private enterprise in Japan's industrialization.

V. RELIGION, EDUCATION, AND THE IMPACT OF WESTERN CULTURE
   A. Early efforts to institutionalize Shinto as state religion and to disestablish Buddhism
   B. Fukuzawa Yukichi (1834–1901), the Meiji Six Society and the Western concept of "progress": emphasis on scientific methods of inquiry; movement for "civilization and enlightenment"; utilitarian, pragmatic, and largely secular attitudes of leaders and intellectuals
   C. Dissemination of information and knowledge: extensive translation of Western literature and technical studies into Japanese; proliferation of vernacular newspapers and periodicals from 1870
   D. Rapid advances in education
      1. Drive for universal literacy: establishment of a national elementary school system (1872); employment of American advisers
      2. Founding of private institutions of higher learning: Keiō University of Fukuzawa Yukichi; Weseda University of Ōkuma Shigenobu; Dōshisha University of Niishima Jō (1843–90)
   E. Reaction to Westernization and beginnings of educational orthodoxy (1880s)
      1. Increased governmental participation in all phases of national education
      2. Added stress on morals courses at elementary school level (1882)
      3. Mori Arinori (1847–89) and Education Act of 1886: aim of education to enhance state, not individual
      4. Imperial Rescript on Education (1890): merging of Emperor, state, and society in Confucian virtues of loyalty and filial piety
      5. Tokyo Imperial University made channel for governmental training and preferment
   F. Debate over Westernization and "preservation of the national essence": Tokutomi Sohō (1863–1957) versus Miyake Setsurei (1860–1945)
   G. Renewal of Christian influence (ban on Christianity removed 1873)
      1. Missionary activities: especially prominent in fields of education, medicine

2. American Protestant teachers, youthful Japanese converts and the doctrine of the "autonomous conscience"
3. Uchimura Kanzō (1861-1930) and the "non-church movement": effort to disengage Christianity from its institutional foundations in Western civilization

Reading Assignments
Beasley, *Modern History*, 134-41, 151-54.
Fairbank, Reischauer, and Craig, *The Modern Transformation*, 261-78.
Sources of Japanese Tradition, 623-37; II, 116-30.

Additional Readings
Blacker, Carmen. *The Japanese Enlightenment: A Study of the Writings of Fukuzawa Yukichi*. Cambridge, England: Cambridge University Press, 1964. Brief, but expertly written, survey of the views of one of the most prominent apostles of "progress" and "Westernization" in Meiji Japan.
Craig, Albert M., "Fukuzawa Yukichi: The Philosophical Foundations of Meiji Nationalism" in Ward (ed.), *Political Development in Modern Japan*. Transitions in Fukuzawa's political and social thought from early infatuation with a "natural order" and optimistic view of evolutionary progress to later uncertainty and greater stress on nationalism and Japan's unique imperial institution. Pp. 99-148.
Hall and Beardsley, *Twelve Doors to Japan*. John W. Hall, "Education and Modern National Development," 384-426. A survey of developments in education from the Tokugawa period until the present.
Jansen, *Changing Japanese Attitudes Toward Modernization*. Donald H. Shively, "Nishimura Shigeki: A Confucian View of Modernization," 193-241; John F. Howes, "Japanese Christians and American Missionaries," 337-68; Shuichi Kato, "Japanese Writers and Modernization," 425-45; Herbert Passin, "Modernization and the Japanese Intellectual: Some Comparative Observations," 447-87.
Kiyooka, Eiichi (tr.). *The Autobiography of Yukichi Fukuzawa*. New York: Columbia University Press, 1966.
Passin, Herbert. *Society and Education in Japan*. New York: Teachers College of Columbia University, 1965. Study of the process of education in modern Japan, its background, its goals, and its

role in Japanese society to the present. Appended are a number of valuable documents on Japanese education.

Pyle, Kenneth B. *The New Generation in Meiji Japan: Problems of Cultural Identity, 1885–1895.* Stanford: Stanford University Press, 1969. Good treatment of the mid-Meiji debate over Western-style progress and Japanese culture between the Spencerian Westernizers, led by Tokutomi Sohō, and those intellectuals advocating "preservation of the national essence."

Sansom, *The Western World and Japan.* Chapters 14 and 15 contain excellent topical essays on literature, thought, law, education, and religion in the Meiji period.

Scheiner, Irwin. *Christian Converts and Social Protest in Meiji Japan.* Berkeley: University of California Press, 1970. Examination of the role of Protestant missionaries and foreign lay teachers in the conversion to Christianity of Japanese youth in the 1870s and 1880s: nurturing of the "autonomous conscience" and its role in mid-Meiji social protest.

Shively, Donald H., "Motoda Eifu: Confucian Lecturer to the Meiji Emperor" in David S. Nivison and Arthur F. Wright (eds.), *Confucianism in Action.* Stanford: Stanford University Press, 1959. This is an important article on an individual close to the Meiji Emperor who devoted his efforts during the years of rapid modernization in the late nineteenth century to the strengthening of the imperial institution and of Confucian ethics in Japanese society.

Shively, Donald (ed.). *Tradition and Modernization in Japanese Culture.* Princeton: Princeton University Press, 1971. Essays on culture, including education, literature, the visual arts and music, in modernizing Japan.

Discussion Topics and Questions
1. Religiosity of the "Meiji Man."
2. Education as a prime factor in Japan's modernization. What priorities did the Japanese adopt in their efforts to develop a modern educational system?
3. The role of Christianity in higher education during the Meiji period.
4. Assess the impact of Christianity on modern Japan.
5. "Eastern morals and western technology": to what extent did the Japanese of the Meiji period use this slogan as their guide?
6. The persistence of Confucian values in modern Japan.

VI. FOUNDING OF CONSTITUTIONAL GOVERNMENT
   A. Preparatory steps
      1. Constitutional study mission, headed by Itō Hirobumi (1841–1909, Chōshū), dispatched to Europe (1882): concentration on German model
      2. Formation of nobility ranks (1884) in preparation for future House of Peers
      3. Founding of a modern Cabinet system (1885): Itō first Prime Minister; nine ministries (foreign, home, finance, war, navy, justice, education, agriculture, and commerce and communications)
      4. Establishment of Privy Council (1888) to review Constitution: Itō first head
   B. Meiji Constitution (1889)
      1. Reaffirmation of imperial sovereignty: Constitution seen as changing form of government (*seitai*), but leaving unaltered Japan's Emperor-centered national polity (*kokutai*)
      2. Bicameral legislature (Diet) consisting of Peers and Representatives with equal lawmaking powers
      3. Position of Cabinet: ministers individually accountable to Emperor; no specified responsibility (transcendental) in relations with Diet
   C. Early Cabinets dominated by oligarchy: evolution of system of selection of Prime Ministers by group of elder statesmen (*genrō*)

Reading Assignments
Beasley, *Modern History*, 126–33.
Fairbank, Reischauer, and Craig, *The Modern Transformation*, 290–98.
Michael and Taylor, *Far East in the Modern World*, 249–57.
Sources of Japanese Tradition, 662–700; II, 155–93.

Additional Readings
Hackett, Roger F., "Political Modernization and the Meiji *Genrō*" in Ward (ed.), *Political Development in Modern Japan*, 65–97.
Linebarger, Paul M. A., Djang Chu, and Ardath W. Burks. *Far Eastern Governments and Politics*. Second edition. New York: Van Nostrand, 1956. Ardath W. Burks, in chapters 16 and 17, provides a carefully considered and provocative discussion of

the Meiji Constitution and its relationship to governmental practice in pre-World War II Japan. Of particular interest is his assertion that the Japanese attempted to *Japanize* Western political ideas and institutions rather than allow such ideas and institutions to *Westernize* their methods of rule.

Miller, Frank O. *Minobe Tatsukichi: Interpreter of Constitutionalism in Japan.* Berkeley and Los Angeles: University of California Press, 1965. An outstanding study of the influence of Western constitutional thought in prewar Japan as reflected in the writings and career of one of the most distinguished legal scholars of the period.

Scalapino, *Democracy and the Party Movement in Prewar Japan.* Chapters 2–4.

Discussion Topics and Questions

1. Why did Germany, in particular, appeal as a model to the authors of the Meiji Constitution?
2. How "appropriate" was the Meiji Constitution as a framework for government within the context of political and social conditions that prevailed in Japan at the time of its promulgation?
3. Opposition of the political parties to transcendental Cabinets.
4. The concept of "national polity" (*kokutai*) in relation to constitutionalism.

VII. TREATY REVISION AND OVERSEAS EXPANSION
A. Achievement of treaty revision (1894; effective 1899)
B. Korean question and Sino-Japanese War (1894–95)
   1. Treaty of Shimonoseki: independence of Korea; cession of Liaotung Peninsula, Formosa, and Pescadores to Japan; indemnity of 200 million *tael* to Japan; opening of treaty ports to Japan
   2. Triple Intervention: Russia, France, and Germany force Japan to retrocede Liaotung Peninsula to China
C. International competition in Northeast Asia: clash of interests with Russia in Korea and Manchuria
   1. American "Open-Door" Policy toward China (1899)
   2. Anglo-Japanese Alliance (1902)
D. Russo-Japanese War (1904–5): Portsmouth Treaty recognizing paramount interests of Japan in Korea and ceding Liaotung Peninsula, southern section of Manchurian Railway, and southern half of Sakhalin to Japan
E. Rapprochement with Russia and annexation of Korea (1910)

Reading Assignments
Beasley, *Modern History*, 155–73.
Fairbank, Reischauer, and Craig, *The Modern Transformation*, 382–84, 477–83.
Michael and Taylor, *Far East in the Modern World*, 153–57, 166–68.

Additional Readings
Conroy, *The Japanese Seizure of Korea, 1868–1910*.
Jones, Francis C. *Extraterritoriality in Japan and the Diplomatic Relations Resulting in Its Abolition, 1853–1899*. New Haven: Yale University Press, 1931. The most detailed account, based on Western language sources, of the problem of the unequal treaties and Japanese efforts to secure their revision.
Langer, William L. *The Diplomacy of Imperialism, 1890–1902*. Two volumes. New York: Knopf, 1935.
Lee, Chong-sik. *The Politics of Korean Nationalism*. Berkeley and Los Angeles: University of California Press, 1965. This book deals with Korean nationalism from its stirrings in the Tonghak Rebellion of 1894 until the end of the Japanese occupation in 1945. It is an excellent case study of colonialism imposed by a non-Western country.

Nish, Ian H. *The Anglo-Japanese Alliance: The Diplomacy of Two Island Empires, 1894–1907.* London: Athlone Press, University of London, 1966. A thoroughly documented account of Anglo-Japanese relations from the Sino-Japanese War through the post-Russo-Japanese War period.

Okamoto, Shumpei. *The Japanese Oligarchy and the Russo-Japanese War.* New York: Columbia University Press, 1970. An exhaustively documented, outstanding analysis of oligarchic decision-making and the failure of the Meiji government to contribute to the cultivation of a responsible public opinion in regard to Japanese foreign policy.

Discussion Topics and Questions
1. Anglo-Japanese Alliance within the context of world diplomacy and strategy among nations in the early years of the twentieth century.
2. Implications and viability of the "Open-Door" Policy as a framework for international relations in the Far East in the pre-World War II period.

VIII. OLIGARCHIC LEADERSHIP OF POLITICAL PARTIES
A. Rivalry between Yamagata Aritomo and Itō Hirobumi
B. Formation of Seiyūkai (1900) : Itō's alignment with party system
C. 1901-13, alternation of premiership between Katsura Tarō (1847-1913) and Saionji Kimmochi (1849-1940)
D. Taishō change (1913) : Katsura's acceptance of need for party affiliation

Reading Assignments
Beasley, *Modern History*, 174-95.
Fairbank, Reischauer, and Craig, *The Modern Transformation*, 299-312, 488-546, 554-61.
Michael and Taylor, *Far East in the Modern World*, 257-63.
Sources of Japanese Tradition, 700-16; II, 193-209.

Additional Readings
Hackett, Roger F. *Yamagata Aritomo in the Rise of Modern Japan, 1838-1922.* Cambridge: Harvard University Press, 1971.
Najita, Tetsuo. *Hara Kei in the Politics of Compromise, 1905-1915.* Cambridge: Harvard University Press, 1967. A distinguished study of the role of Hara as the true builder of Japan's first modern party through compromise with the existing power structure rather than appeal for mass support.
Scalapino, *Democracy and the Party Movement in Prewar Japan*, Chapter 5.

Discussion Topics and Questions
1. What were the roots of division within the oligarchy ca. 1900: civilian versus military; Itō versus Yamagata?
2. Emergence of a new ruling elite in the Taishō period. Compare it to the former Meiji elite (oligarchy) in terms of background, aims, methods, etc.

IX. WORLD WAR I
  A. Occupation of German possessions in China and Pacific (1914)
  B. "Twenty-one Demands" (1915)
     1. Call for territorial and commercial concessions from China
     2. World opinion turns against Japan
     3. Japan forced to withdraw Group V "wishes"
  C. Preoccupation of Western nations with European war: new markets and economic prosperity for Japan in East Asia
  D. Diplomacy of Terauchi Masatake (1852–1919)
     1. Nishihara loans to China
     2. Siberian intervention
     3. International negotiations in preparation for peace treaty
  E. Rice riots and fall of Terauchi Cabinet (Sept. 1918)
  F. Treaty of Versailles (1919)
     1. Settlement of interests in China
     2. Pacific island mandates

Reading Assignments
Beasley, *Modern History,* 196–210.
Fairbank, Reischauer, and Craig, *The Modern Transformation,* 561–68.
Michael and Taylor, *Far East in the Modern World,* 275–78.
Sources of Japanese Tradition, 716–17; II, 209–10.

Additional Readings
MacNair, Harley F., and Donald F. Lach. *Modern Far Eastern International Relations.* Second edition. New York: Van Nostrand, 1955. One of several comprehensive studies of modern international relations in the Far East. Chapter 7, on World War I, includes a detailed discussion of the Twenty-one Demands.
Morley, James W. *The Japanese Thrust Into Siberia.* New York: Columbia University Press, 1957. Well-documented study of Japan's intervention in Siberia. Especially valuable for an understanding of Japanese policymaking in the World War I period.

X. INAUGURATION OF "RESPONSIBLE PARTY GOVERNMENT": TAISHŌ DEMOCRACY

A. Cabinet of Hara Kei (1856–1921), first "commoner" Prime Minister: but failure to support universal manhood suffrage; increase in military budget
B. Movement to "Protect the Constitution" and Cabinet of Katō Kōmei (1860–1926): passage of universal manhood suffrage and Peace Preservation Law (1925)
C. Intellectual spokesmen for responsible party government: Minobe Tatsukichi (1873–1948) and Yoshino Sakuzō (1878–1933)
D. Two-party system (Seiyūkai and Minseitō): general acceptance of principle of alternation according to party pluralities in House of Representatives
E. Economic enterprise during 1920s
 1. Concentration of industrial power in *zaibatsu* (big four: Mitsui, Mitsubishi, Yasuda, Sumitomo)
 2. Continuance of "dual economy": traditional and modern industries in juxtaposition
 3. General economic stagnation

Reading Assignments
Beasley, *Modern History*, 214–28.
Fairbank, Reischauer, and Craig, *The Modern Transformation*, 568–77.
Michael and Taylor, *Far East in the Modern World*, 523–42.
Sources of Japanese Tradition, 718–53; II, 211–46.

Additional Readings
Duus, Peter. *Party Rivalry and Political Change in Taishō Japan.* Cambridge: Harvard University Press, 1968. Study of the evolution of a two-party system and commencement of the era of party government.

Discussion Topics and Questions
1. Was Hara Kei a "liberal"?
2. To what extent had the Japanese established democratic institutions and democratic patterns of behavior by the 1920s?
3. Crucial questions affecting the development and success of liberal democracy in Japan (cf. Yoshino Sakuzō).

XI. THE LEFT WING IN JAPANESE POLITICS: DIVISION AND SUPPRESSION
 A. Ōi Kentarō (1843–1922) and socialist stirrings as radical offshoot from early party movement
 B. Following Sino-Japanese War
  1. Emergence of organized socialist movement as result of factory shutdowns and unemployment
  2. Establishment of Socialist-Democratic Party (1901) : Abe Isō (1865–1949), Katayama Sen (1859–1933) and others
 C. Following Russo-Japanese War
  1. Embryonic demands for abolition of class system, nationalization of means of production, equal distribution of wealth, universal manhood suffrage
  2. Government suppression and growing division within socialist movement over parliamentary versus revolutionary means: anarchism of Kōtoku Shūsui (1871–1911) and plot to assassinate Meiji Emperor, 1910–11
 D. Following World War I: economic disequilibrium and renewed social agitation
  1. Spread of left-wing doctrines, ranging from parliamentary socialism to communism
  2. Reasons for failure of left-wing movement
   a. Greater appeal to intellectuals than to masses
   b. Tactical and ideological disputes; factionalism; instabiliy of "popular front" coalitions
   c. Difficulty of organizing labor: paternalism in industry; plethora of small firms; surplus of workers; ties to families in countryside
   d. Nationalism effectively monopolized by right wing
   e. Continuing government suppression

Reading Assignments
Beasley, *Modern History,* 228–35.
Fairbank, Reischauer, and Craig, *The Modern Transformation,* 546–54.
Michael and Taylor, *Far East in the Modern World,* 516–19.
Sources of Japanese Tradition, 806–44; II, 299–337.

Additional Readings
Jansen, Marius B. "Ōi Kentarō's Radicalism and Chauvinism," *Far Eastern Quarterly,* XI, no. 3 (1952), 305–16.

Kublin, Hyman. *Asian Revolutionary: The Life of Sen Katayama*. Princeton: Princeton University Press, 1964.

Notehelfer, F. G. *Kōtoku Shūsui, Portrait of a Japanese Radical*. London: Cambridge University Press, 1971. A study of the evolution of Kōtoku's thought within the context of his traditional background, personal psychological make-up, and exposure to modern Western ideologies.

Scalapino, *Democracy and the Party Movement in Prewar Japan*. Chapter 8, "The Rise and Decline of the Left," 294-345.

Totten, George O. *The Social Democratic Movement in Prewar Japan*. New Haven: Yale University Press, 1966. This book contains a wealth of information on prewar left-wing groups, their organization, leadership, and policies. It is probably best used as a reference work. See especially Chapter 1, "The Inhospitable Environment," 3-38; Chapter 8, "Class Concepts and Strategy and Tactics," 179-206; and Chapter 15, "Characteristics of Japanese Social Democracy," 381-402.

Discussion Topics and Questions

1. Leftist ideological disputes in prewar Japan: mass versus class appeal; evolutionary versus revolutionary strategy; legal versus illegal tactics.
2. The problem of factionalism: to what extent a feature of Japanese society as a whole? to what extent peculiar to the left-wing movement?
3. Nationalism and socialism.

XII. FOREIGN POLICY IN THE 1920s
A. International agreements on the Far East
1. Washington Conference (1921–22) : United States initiative; accompanied by termination of Anglo-Japanese Alliance
   a. Four-Power Treaty on Insular Possessions (France, Great Britain, Japan, United States) : recognition of existing rights in Pacific
   b. Five-Power Naval Disarmament Treaty: ratio on maintenance of capital ships (Great Britain 5, United States 5, Japan 3, France 1.75, Italy 1.75)
   c. Nine-Power Treaty (Belgium, China, France, Great Britain, Italy, Japan, Netherlands, Portugal, United States) : reiteration of principles of the Open Door toward China
2. London Naval Treaty (1930) : extension of 5:5:3 ratio for Great Britain, Japan, and United States to non-capital ships
B. Shidehara Kijūrō (1872–1951) as Foreign Minister: participation in "economic diplomacy"; maintenance of status quo through international cooperation; development of markets in China
C. Tanaka Giichi (1863–1929) as Prime Minister: military intervention in China

Reading Assignments
Beasley, *Modern History,* 210–13.
Fairbank, Reischauer, and Craig, *The Modern Transformation:* see Reading Assignments for Section X.
Sources of Japanese Tradition, 753–58; II, 246–51.

Additional Readings
Crowley, James B. *Japan's Quest for Autonomy.* Princeton: Princeton University Press, 1967. A detailed and interpretive study of Japanese foreign policy in the pre-World War II period. Pp. 3–81 provide the historical setting and a discussion of the Washington and London naval treaties.
Iriye, Akira. *After Imperialism: The Search for a New Order in the Far East, 1921–1931.* Cambridge: Harvard University Press, 1965. Atheneum Paperback, 1969. The author of this study of foreign affairs has attempted to assess, through primary sources in several languages, the roles of each of the major countries—China,

Japan, the United States, England, and the Soviet Union—who sought a new working order or balance of power in the Far East during the post-World War I period.

Discussion Topics and Questions
1. End of "diplomacy of imperialism" and Japan's participation in "economic diplomacy" of the 1920s.
2. Comparison of Shidehara and Tanaka policies in the post-World War I period.

XIII. GROWTH OF THE RIGHT WING: EMPEROR-CENTERED NATIONALISM AND MILITARY ACTIVISM

A. Early nationalist movement of the Meiji period: continuation of expansionist ideals of 1873 War Party
  1. Gen'yōsha (Dark Ocean Society)
     a. Founded 1881 in Fukuoka, Kyushu, by Tōyama Mitsuru (1855–1944) and others
     b. Spy activities in Korea: gathering of information for Sino-Japanese War
  2. Kokuryūkai (Amur River Society)
     a. Successor to Gen'yōsha: founded 1900 by Uchida Ryōhei (1874–1937)
     b. Spy and information-gathering activities on continent in preparation for Russo-Japanese War
  3. Support given to Chinese revolutionaries leading to overthrow of Manchu Dynasty (1911–12)
B. Proliferation of nationalist societies from end of World War I: reaction to foreign ideologies and desire to revive traditional values; largely civilian participation
  1. Gondō Seikei (1868–1937): call for return to agrarian primitivism
  2. Kita Ikki (1883–1937): revolutionary nationalism; plans for reorganization of state (national socialism)
  3. Ōkawa Shūmei (1886–1957): reaffirmation of conservative nationalism (Japanism)

Reading Assignments
Beasley, *Modern History:* see Reading Assignments for XVI.
Fairbank, Reischauer, and Craig, *The Modern Transformation:* see Reading Assignments for Section XVI.
Michael and Taylor, *Far East in the Modern World,* 520–23.
Sources of Japanese Tradition, 759–98; II, 252–91.

Additional Readings
Brown, Delmer M. *Nationalism in Japan.* Berkeley and Los Angeles: University of California Press, 1955. A survey of Japanese nationalism from the beginnings of "national consciousness" in ancient times to the post-World War I period.
Jansen, Marius B. *The Japanese and Sun Yat-sen.* Cambridge: Harvard University Press, 1954. Stanford Paperback, 1970. A

scholarly study of the origins of modern Japanese nationalism and early expansionist activities on the Asian mainland.

Maruyama Masao. *Thought and Behavior in Modern Japanese Politics.* Ivan Morris (ed.). London: Oxford University Press, 1963. Paperback (expanded), 1969. A collection of translated essays, by one of Japan's leading political scientists, on prewar "ultranationalism," "fascism," the behavior of wartime leaders, etc.

Storry, Richard. *The Double Patriots.* Boston: Houghton Mifflin, 1957. Although more recent studies, based on a wider range of source materials, are adding new dimensions to our understanding of Japan's prewar nationalist phase, this remains an important work on the stormy decade of the 1930s. Chapters 1-3 deal with nationalism up to 1930.

Wilson, George M. *Radical Nationalist in Japan: Kita Ikki, 1883-1937.* Cambridge: Harvard University Press, 1969. Biographical sketch of one of the leading nationalist intellectuals in Japan before World War II.

Discussion Topics and Questions

1. The Emperor System and modern Japanese nationalism.
2. Composition of nationalist groups to 1930: what classes and sectors of society were represented?
3. Importance of samurai tradition in the right-wing movement from its origins in the early Meiji period.
4. The critique of liberalism and bourgeois values by ultranationalists; of capitalism and bureaucratism.

XIV. DEVELOPMENT OF A MODERN LITERATURE

A. Translation, from 1860s, of European novels and poetry: growing interest in new forms, freer styles of expression, imagery from everyday life
B. Assertion of fiction as independent art: Tsubouchi Shōyō (1859–1935) and *The Essence of the Novel* (1885)
  1. Reaction against traditional didacticism
  2. New concern with realism, plot development, and characterization: personal novels, autobiographical themes
C. Futabatei Shimei (1864–1909) and *The Drifting Cloud* (1887–89) : first true modern novel; use of vernacular language
D. Perfection of the novel: Natsume Sōseki (1867–1916) and *Kokoro* (representative work available in English translation)
E. Continuation of traditional sense of fiction: stress on the intuitive, the evocative
  1. Nagai Kafū (1879–1959) and *The River Sumida* (representative work available in English translation)
  2. Kawabata Yasunari (1899–) and *Snow Country* (representative work available in English translation)
F. Tanizaki Junichirō (1886–1965)
  1. *Some Prefer Nettles:* isolation of modern man; pull of East and West
  2. *The Makioka Sisters:* study of prewar Japan as a dying society

Reading Assignments
Fairbank, Reischauer, and Craig, *The Modern Transformation:* see Reading Assignments for Section VIII.

Additional Readings
Kawabata Yasunari. *Snow Country.* Translated with an introduction by Edward G. Seidensticker. New York: Knopf, 1956.
Keene, Donald. *Modern Japanese Literature.* New York: Grove Press, 1956. Paperback, 1960. Translated selections from the works of many of the most prominent writers of modern Japan.
Morris, Ivan (ed.). *Modern Japanese Stories: An Anthology.* Rutland, Vermont, and Tokyo: Tuttle, 1962.
Natsume Sōseki. *Kokoro.* Translated with an introduction by

Edwin McClellan. Chicago: Regnery, 1957. Gateway Paperback, 1967.

Ryan, Marleigh G. *Japan's First Modern Novel: Ukigumo of Futabatei Shimei.* New York: Columbia University Press, 1967. Paperback, 1971. Futabatei's pioneer work in translation with an extensive introduction on the man, his work, and his times.

Seidensticker, Edward. *Kafū the Scribbler: The Life and Writings of Nagai Kafū, 1879–1959.* Stanford: Stanford University Press, 1965. Paperback, 1968. A sensitively written study of an important modern writer; with selected translations from his works.

Shively, *Tradition and Modernization in Japanese Culture.* See essays by Hibbett, McClellan, Brower, and Seidensticker on modern literature.

Discussion Topics and Questions

1. Elements of continuity in Japan's traditional and modern prose fiction.
2. Women in modern Japanese literature—e.g., compare the heroines of Kawabata and Tanizaki.

XV. THE VISUAL ARTS IN THE MODERN AGE
A. On the eve of the Meiji Restoration
 1. Trend toward Western-style realism in landscape prints of Hokusai (1760–1849) and Hiroshige (1797–1858)
 2. General decline in traditional forms of art (painting, ink drawings, woodblock prints, etc.) in final years of Tokugawa period
B. Early Meiji period: craze for Western artistic styles and aesthetic principles; rejection of native art
C. Ernest Fenollosa (1853–1908), Okakura Tenshin (1862–1913) and the movement (from ca. 1878) to reaffirm Japan's artistic tradition
D. Twentieth-century trends
 1. Continuing problem of choice between Western and Oriental idioms; tendency toward "internationalization" of Japanese art
 2. Revival in popularity of woodblock prints by modern artists
 3. Japan's leading role in ceramics
 4. Influence of Japan on architecture and industrial design throughout world (especially significant in post-world War II period)

Additional Readings
Munsterberg, *The Arts of Japan*. There is, regrettably, very little textual material on the visual arts in Japan since the Meiji Restoration. The author of this survey work is one of the few who devotes more than a few words to modern trends. See 169–86.
Sansom, *The Western World and Japan*. The section on "Popular Sentiment" in Chapter 14 ("Early Meiji: Western Influences") gives the setting for the Japanese reaction to western art in the Meiji period.
Shively, *Tradition and Modernization in Japanese Culture*. See John M. Rosenfield, "Western-Style Painting in the Early Meiji Period and Its Critics"; Tōru Haga, "The Formation of Realism in Meiji Painting: The Artistic Career of Takahashi Yuichi."
Statler, Oliver. *Modern Japanese Prints: An Art Reborn*. Rutland, Vermont, and Tokyo: Tuttle, 1956. Brief portraits of the leading print artists of modern Japan; abundantly illustrated.

XVI. WORLD DEPRESSION AND MILITARY ADVENTURISM ON THE CONTINENT
  A. Cabinet of Hamaguchi Osachi (1870–1931)
    1. Return to Shidehara diplomacy and international cooperation
    2. London Naval Treaty and dispute over violation of "prerogative of supreme command"
    3. Return to gold standard and collapse of world market
  B. Conspiracies against the government: March and October (1931) plots involving Sakurakai (Cherry Society)
  C. Manchurian Incident (Sept. 1931) : "dual diplomacy" and aggression in China; *fait accompli* attitude toward territorial expansion

Reading Assignments
Beasley, *Modern History*, 236–46.
Fairbank, Reischauer, and Craig, *The Modern Transformation*, 577–88.
Michael and Taylor, *Far East in the Modern World*, 542–57.
Sources of Japanese Tradition: see Reading Assignments for Section XIII.

Additional Readings
Ogata, Sadako N. *Defiance in Manchuria: The Making of Japanese Foreign Policy, 1931–1932.* Berkeley and Los Angeles: University of California Press, 1964. Covers in detail the Manchurian Incident up through the founding of the state of Manchukuo.
Storry, *The Double Patriots.* Chapter 4, "The Manchurian Incident."

XVII. PERIOD OF TERRORISM, CONSPIRACY, AND ASSASSINATION, MAY 1932–FEBRUARY 1936: transfer of initiative in ultranationalist activities from civilian to military; call for a "Shōwa Restoration"; expansion on the continent
   A. Ketsumeidan (Blood Brotherhood) and May 15 Incident (1932) : assassination of Prime Minister Inukai Tsuyoshi (1855–1932) by "young officers"; end of party government
   B. Founding of Manchukuo (1932) and withdrawal from League of Nations (1933)
   C. Minobe Tatsukichi and debate over "emperor-organ" theory: suppression of unorthodox views
   D. Intra-army faction dispute
      1. Kōdō (Imperial Way) Faction: emphasis on spiritual values of Japanese Army
      2. Tōsei (Control) Faction: for rationalization of Army through stress on modern equipment, economic planning, etc.
      3. Climax of faction dispute: February 26 Mutiny (1936)
   E. Publication of *Kokutai no Hongi* (Fundamentals of our national polity) and enforcement of orthodox nationalist thought (1937)

Reading Assignments
Beasley, *Modern History*, 246–57.
Fairbank, Reischauer, and Craig, *The Modern Transformation*, 588–97.
Michael and Taylor, *Far East in the Modern World*, 557–62.
Sources of Japanese Tradition: see Reading Assignments for Section XIII.

Additional Readings
Crowley, *Japan's Quest for Autonomy*. This study of Japanese foreign policy, 1930–38, is particularly interesting for the information it contains on the Army faction struggle that culminated in the February 26, 1936 Mutiny.
Hall, Robert K. (ed.). *Kokutai no Hongi: Cardinal Principles of the National Entity of Japan*. Translated by John O. Gauntlett. Cambridge: Harvard University Press, 1949.
Miller, *Minobe Tatsukichi: Interpreter of Constitutionalism in Japan*. Cited under VI above. Chapter 7 deals with "The Minobe Affair."

Schumpeter. E. B. (ed.). *The Industrialization of Japan and Manchukuo 1930–1940*. New York: Macmillan, 1940. An exhaustive study of various aspects of the prewar economy of the Japanese Empire.

Storry, *The Double Patriots,* 96–191.

Discussion Topics and Questions
1. To what extent, if at all, is it appropriate to label Japanese political behavior during the 1930s as "fascist"?
2. Issues involved in debate over the "emperor-organ" theory: Minobe's legalism versus the irrationalism of his opponents; Minobe the critic as a real threat to the aspirations of the military.
3. The critique of other ideologies in *Kokutai no Hongi:* the conception of Japan's mission in Asia and the world.

XVIII. THE PACIFIC WAR, 1937-1945
- A. Marco Polo Bridge Incident and beginning of hostilities with China (July 1937)
- B. Gradual formation of a militarist state in Japan
  1. Establishment of boards for policy planning and coordination of Service activities
  2. Economic management through government controls
  3. Dissolution of political parties
  4. Efforts at "spiritual mobilization"
- C. Prime Minister Konoe Fumimaro (1891-1945) and announcement of a "New Order in East Asia" (Nov. 1938)
- D. Establishment of Nanking puppet government under Wang Ching-wei (March 1940)
- E. Matsuoka Yōsuke (1880-1946) and Tripartite (Axis) Pact with Germany and Italy (1940)
- F. Growing tensions in the Pacific: Cabinet of Tōjō Hideki (1884-1948) and decision to attack United States
- G. Japan in World War II (1941-45)

Reading Assignments
Beasley, *Modern History,* 258-78.
Fairbank, Reischauer, and Craig, *The Modern Transformation,* 597-612, 804-11.
Michael and Taylor, *Far East in the Modern World,* 563-84.
Sources of Japanese Tradition, 798-805; II, 291-98.

Additional Readings
Butow, Robert J. C. *Japan's Decision To Surrender.* Stanford: Stanford University Press, 1954. Paperback, 1967. A fascinating account of the maneuvering among Japanese leaders in the final days of the war that led to acceptance of the Potsdam surrender terms.
Butow, Robert J. C. *Tojo and the Coming of the War.* Princeton: Princeton University Press, 1961. Stanford Paperback, 1969.
Feis, Herbert. *The Atomic Bomb and the End of World War II.* Princeton: Princeton University Press, 1966. This is essentially an account of American decision-making in the final stages of the war with Japan.
Feis, Herbert. *The Road to Pearl Harbor.* Princeton: Princeton University Press, 1950.

Jones, F. C. *Japan's New Order in East Asia.* London: Oxford University Press, 1954. A detailed study of international relations in the Far East, 1937-45, based on materials in Western languages, including the records of the International Military Tribunal held in Tokyo, 1946-48.

Discussion Topics and Questions
1. The context of international relations that led to Japan's entry into the Axis Pact.
2. What, precisely, were Japan's aims and aspirations in seeking to establish a "new order" and a "co-prosperity sphere" in East Asia?

XIX. DEFEAT AND OCCUPATION, 1945–1952

A. Surrender to Allied Powers (August–September 1945) in accordance with Potsdam Declaration: acceptance of allied occupation; loss of overseas empire, including Korea, Manchuria, Formosa, Pescadores, and Pacific islands

B. Period of demilitarization and democratization (1945–47)
 1. Initiative and general conduct of occupation assumed by United States: Douglas MacArthur appointed Supreme Commander for Allied Powers (SCAP); SCAP policies implemented through Japanese government
 2. Demilitarization: dismantling of military installations and elimination of war-making potential; purge of former military and business leaders; war crimes trials; disestablishment of State Shinto
 3. Adoption of new constitution (in form of amendment to Meiji Constitution) under SCAP direction (May 1947)
   a. Sovereignty vested in people
   b. Emperor a "symbol of state"
   c. British-style relationship between Cabinet and Diet (hence strengthening of legislature vis-à-vis executive)
   d. Fully elective House of Representatives and House of Councilors
   e. Guarantees of human rights
   f. Independence of judiciary
   g. Outlawing of war (Article IX)
 4. Reforms in land, labor, education, police; economic deconcentration program (*zaibatsu*-busting)

C. Period of recovery (1948–52)
 1. Measures by SCAP to encourage economic recovery: relaxation of purges and reversal of industrial deconcentration program; removal of restrictions to foreign trade
 2. San Francisco Peace Treaty between Japan and major noncommunist belligerents (1951)
 3. Impetus given economy by United States spending during Korean War (1950–53)

Reading Assignments
Beasley, *Modern History,* 279–304.

Fairbank, Reischauer, and Craig, *The Modern Transformation*, 811–21.
Michael and Taylor, *Far East in the Modern World*, 584–95.

Additional Readings

Dore, Ronald P. *Land Reform in Japan*. London: Oxford University Press, 1959. A study of the postwar land reform with an extensive introductory section devoted to the prewar agrarian setting.

Kawai, Kazuo. *Japan's American Interlude*. Chicago: University of Chicago Press, 1960. The most readable account of the American Occupation of Japan. Contains much valuable information on modern Japanese attitudes and behavior.

Passin, Herbert (ed.). *The United States and Japan*. Englewood Cliffs, New Jersey: Prentice-Hall, 1966. A collection of essays on Japan today, with the focus on ties with the United States. See Robert E. Ward, "The Legacy of the Occupation," 29–56.

Discussion Topics and Questions

1. Effect of purges on political and business leadership in Japan; degree of continuity or discontinuity between prewar and postwar elites.
2. Reasons for SCAP's "reverse course" policy from around 1948: domestic conditions in Japan; international pressures.

XX. INDEPENDENCE AND ECONOMIC PROSPERITY
  A. Political balance: "one and a half" party system
     1. Liberal-Democratic Party: ruling conservative coalition, maintaining approximately two-thirds support of electorate
     2. Socialist Party: perennial opposition force in Diet; wide range of ideological positions, merging with Communist Party on far left
  B. Foreign relations and military defense
     1. Reliance on Mutual Security Treaty with United States for military defense; issue of national rearmament and "anti-war" clause in Constitution
     2. Problem of regularization of relations with Communist China, Korea, and Russia
     3. Demands for termination of United States occupation of Okinawa (terminated 1972) and for return of Kuriles from Russia
     4. Participation in United Nations, but reluctance to assume role in international relations commensurate with stature as great industrial nation
  C. Continuing economic resurgence and prosperity
     1. Preponderance of trade with United States: sensitivity to American economic fluctuations and tariff policies
     2. Development of new export markets for high-quality manufactured goods: cameras, electronic equipment, precision instruments, etc.
  D. Intellectual and spiritual atmosphere
     1. New freedom of expression: reaction against traditional beliefs and search for new values; stress on Japanese "technology" rather than prewar-type "unique national spirit"; anti-war sentiments
     2. Popularity of "new religions": search for happiness on earth; simplicity of doctrines; special importance of Sōka Gakkai (Value Creation Society) as religious and political movement
     3. Widespread quest for leisure in 1960s

Reading Assignments
Beasley, *Modern History:* see Reading Assignments for Section XIX; also 305–19.
Fairbank, Reischauer, and Craig, *The Modern Transformation,* 821–43.

Michael and Taylor, *Far East in the Modern World*, 595–614.
Sources of Japanese Tradition, 845–906; II, 338–99.

Additional Readings

Allen, G. C. *Japan's Economic Expansion*. London: Oxford University Press, 1965. An up-to-date, topical study of Japan's postwar economy.

Dore, R. P. (ed.). *Aspects of Social Change in Modern Japan*. Princeton: Princeton University Press, 1967. Paperback, 1971. The essays in this book cover a variety of topics, with background material, on social change in modern Japan. The book is appropriately cited here because its focus is essentially on present-day Japan. Of particular value for the general student are two essays in Part Two, "Mobility and Migration": Ezra F. Vogel, "Kinship Structure, Migration to the City, and Modernization"; and R. P. Dore, "Mobility, Equality, and Individuation in Modern Japan."

Dore, R. P. *City Life in Japan: A Study of a Tokyo Ward*. Berkeley and Los Angeles: University of California Press, 1958. Paperback, 1965. This is a lengthy and detailed study of urban society in modern Japan.

Lockwood, *The State and Economic Enterprise in Japan*. See Part Three, "Growth, Stability, and Welfare in Japan Today."

Morris, Ivan I. *Nationalism and the Right Wing in Japan: A Study of Post-war Trends*. London: Oxford University Press, 1960.

Nakane, Chie. *Japanese Society*. Berkeley: University of California Press, 1970. Brief, excellent analysis of Japanese behavior.

Packard, George R. *Protest in Tokyo: The Security Crisis of 1960*. Princeton: Princeton University Press, 1966. This is the most important political case study on the postwar period.

Passin, *The United States and Japan*. Lawrence Olson, "Political Relations," 57–91; William Lockwood, "Political Economy," 93–127; Herbert Passin, "The Future," 141–61.

Scalapino, Robert A. *The Japanese Communist Movement, 1920–1966*. Berkeley and Los Angeles: University of California Press, 1967. Primarily a study of the communist movement in the post-World War II period.

Scalapino, Robert A., "The United States and Japan" in Willard L. Thorp (ed.), *The United States and the Far East*. Englewood Cliffs, New Jersey: Prentice-Hall, 1962. Pp. 11–73. A perceptive overview of American-Japanese relations from the time of Perry to the present.

Scalapino, Robert A., and Junnosuke Masumi. *Parties and Politics in Contemporary Japan*. Berkeley and Los Angeles: University of California Press, 1962. Paperback, 1965. A good discussion of the Japanese political process; with a case study of the 1960 crisis over revision of the security treaty with the United States.

Thayer, Nathaniel B. *How the Conservatives Rule Japan*. Princeton: Princeton University Press, 1969.

Thomsen, Harry. *The New Religions of Japan*. Rutland, Vermont and Tokyo: Tuttle, 1963. Useful survey of the new religions with data on their founding, background, composition, etc.

Vogel, Ezra F. *Japan's New Middle Class: The Salary Man and His Family in a Tokyo Suburb*. Berkeley and Los Angeles: University of California Press, 1963. Paperback, 1967. Highly recommended for an understanding of family life and social behavior in postwar Japan.

Discussion Questions and Topics

1. Implications of Japan's failure to develop a "political center" in the postwar period; future of the two-party system.
2. Issues and ideological positions involved in the call for constitutional amendment; the larger question of the continued acceptability of a foreign-imposed Constitution.
3. Communism in the Japanese setting. The Japan Communist Party's position in regard to the Sino-Soviet split.
4. Present and possible future attitudes of the Japanese toward the imperial institution.
5. Japan's national identity and cultural identity in the postwar world.
6. The significance of the "new religions." How "new" are they? To what needs do they respond?

MAPS

MAP I
FAMOUS CITIES AND
PLACES IN JAPANESE HIST
S
TSUSHIMA
Hakata Bay
Dan-no-ura
Hiroshima
Nagasaki
INLAND
SEA
KYUSHU
SHIKOK
TANEGASHIMA

MAP II
MITO AND THE GREAT WESTER
OF THE LATE TOKUGUWA PE
S
CHŌSHŪ
HIZEN
SATSUMA
TOSA

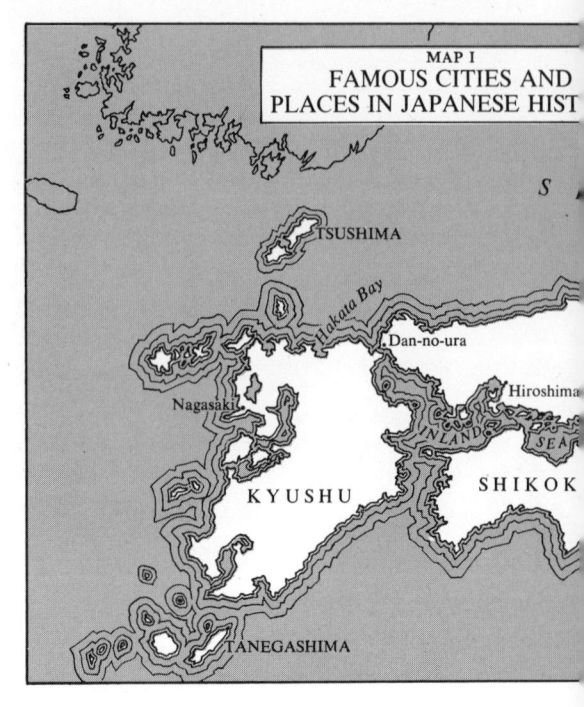

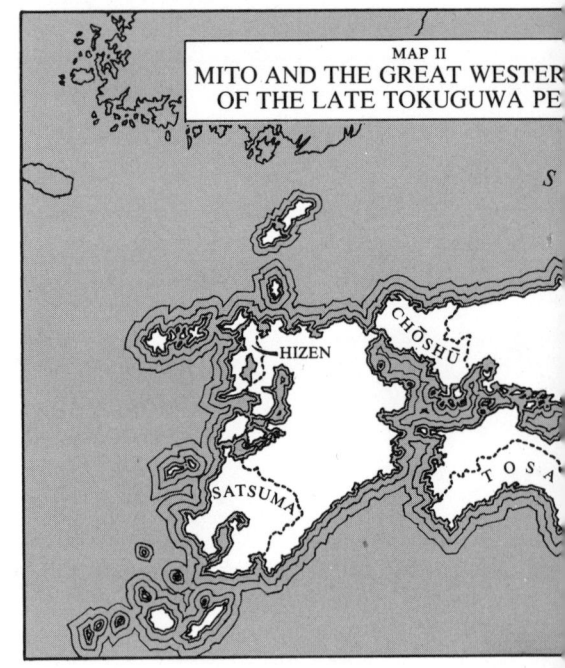

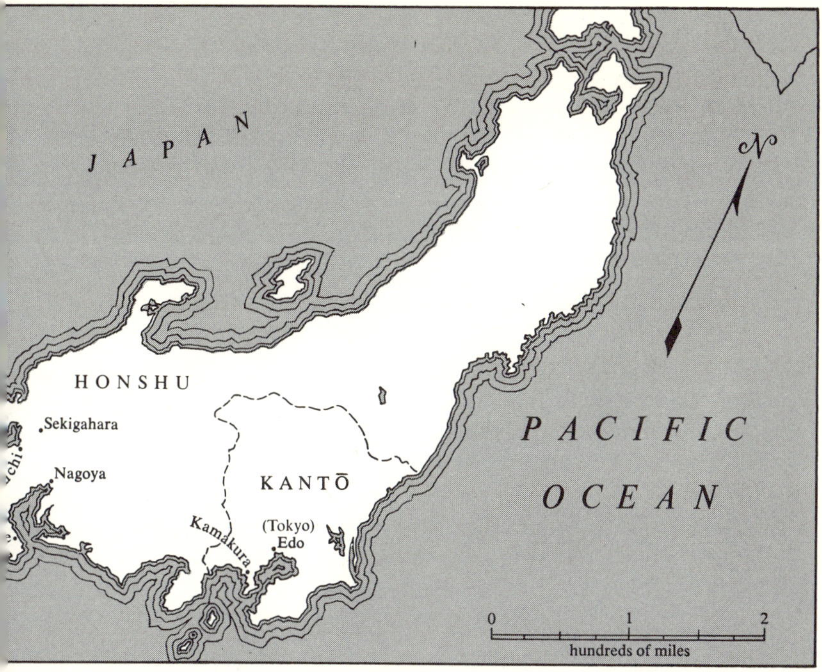

Map 1

JAPAN

HONSHU
- Sekigahara
- Nagoya
- Kamakura
- KANTŌ
- (Tokyo) Edo

PACIFIC OCEAN

0 — 1 — 2 hundreds of miles

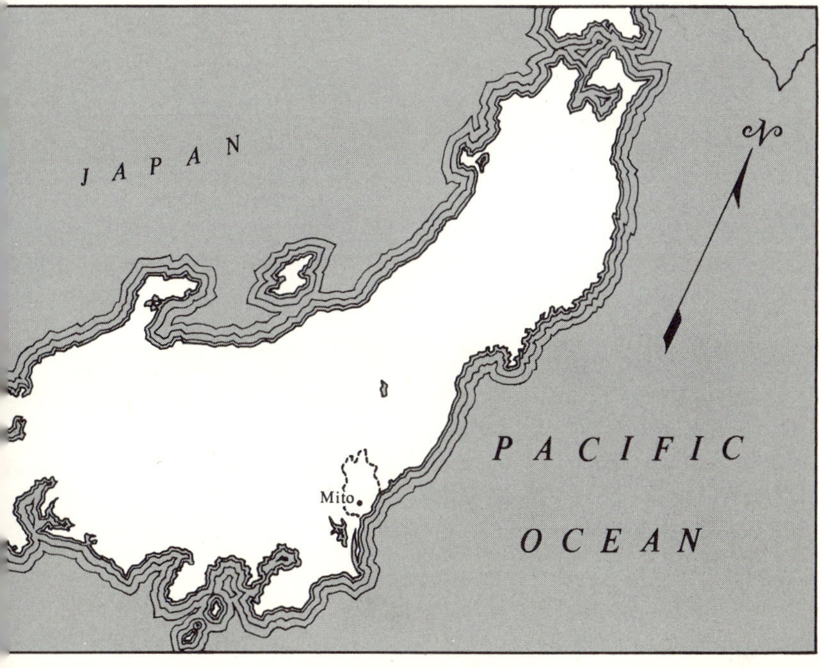

Map 2

JAPAN

- Mito

PACIFIC OCEAN

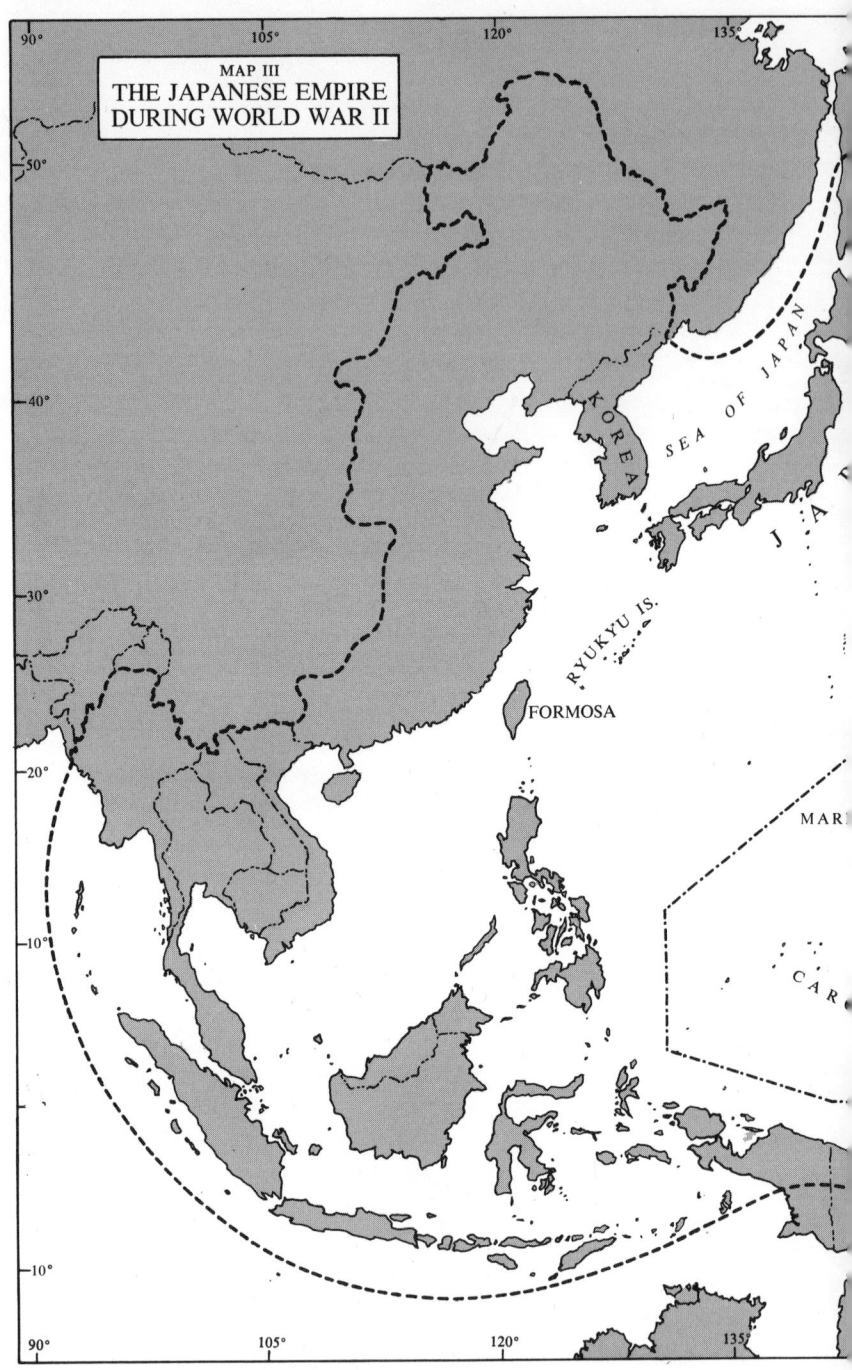

After a map in M. I. T. Series Strategic Area Maps. Copyright by Massachusetts Institute of Technolo

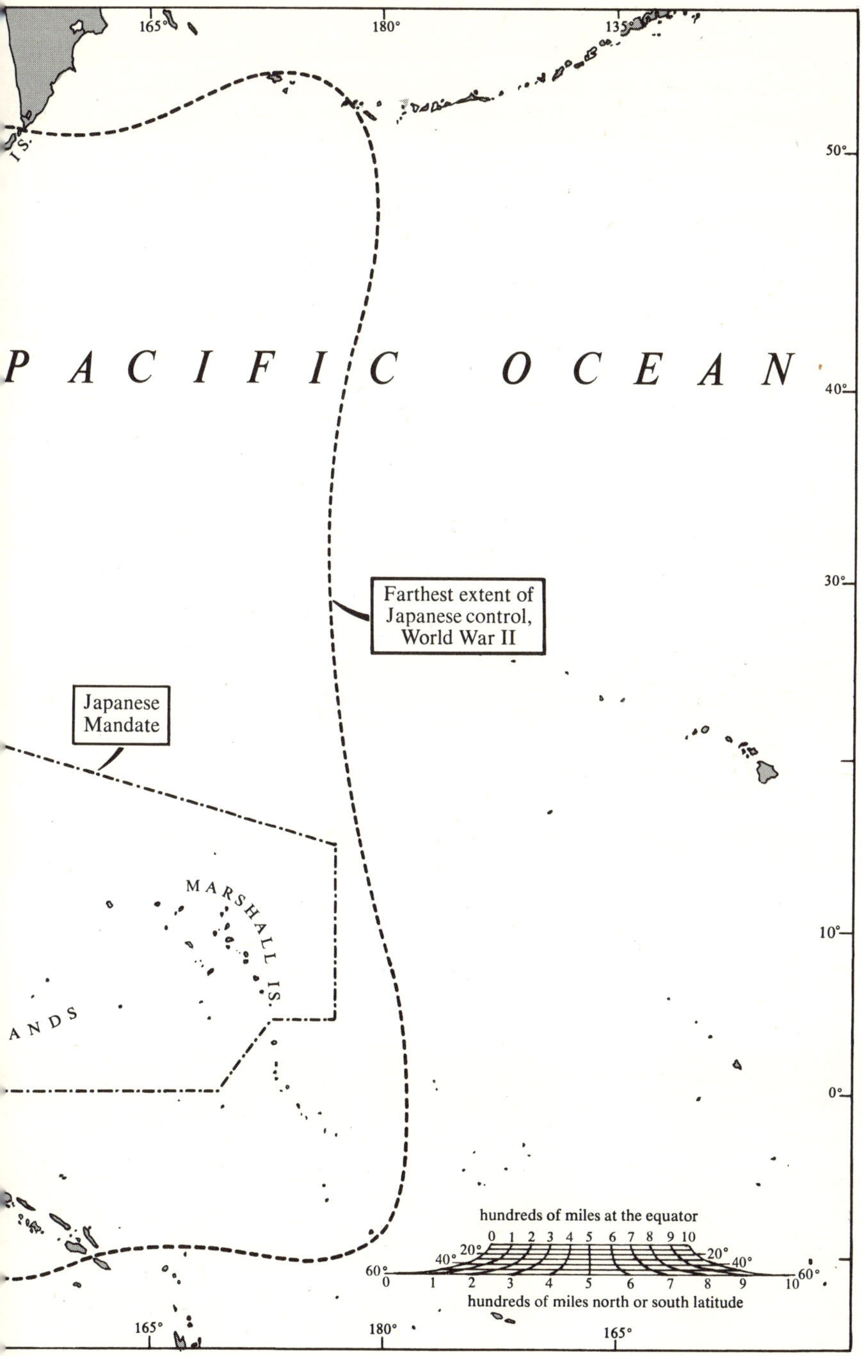
165°
180°
135°
IS.
50°
P A C I F I C O C E A N
40°
30°
Farthest extent of Japanese control, World War II
Japanese Mandate
MARSHALL IS.
ANDS
10°
0°
hundreds of miles at the equator
0 1 2 3 4 5 6 7 8 9 10
20°
40°
60°
0 1 2 3 4 5 6 7 8 9 10
hundreds of miles north or south latitude
165°
180°
165°

PRONUNCIATION GUIDE

Japanese words and names have been transcribed in this syllabus according to the Hepburn system of Romanization. Vowels in Japanese are similar to those in Italian:

a	as in	arm
i	as the first *e* in	eve
u	as in	rude
e	as the *a* in	chaotic
o	as in	old

Long marks or macrons over the vowels *u* and *o* (*ū*, *ō*) require that the sound be held for twice its normal duration.* Since there are no true diphthongs in Japanese, each vowel must be pronounced separately. For example, the word *kai* is pronounced *ka-i*.

Consonants are pronounced as in English (*g* is always hard) with the exception of *r*, which is rendered like the unrolled *r* of Spanish. Double consonants should be sustained in the same fashion as the lengthened vowels mentioned above.

* The long marks are usually omitted from such prominent place names as Tokyo, Kyoto, Osaka, Honshu, Kyushu, and Hokkaido.

GLOSSARY OF TERMS

AWARE An aesthetic term which, over the centuries, has developed a range of meanings from "sensitivity" to sadness to the present-day connotation of wretchedness or grief.

BAKUFU Premodern military government or shogunate.

BE Groups in early Japanese society organized along occupational lines—e.g., farmers, fishermen, pottery makers.

BUSHIDŌ "Way of the Warrior." A phrase, usually attributed to Yamaga Sokō (1622–85), connoting the ideals of the samurai class.

FUDAI DAIMYŌ Daimyos who were hereditary vassals of the Tokugawa House on the basis of vows taken before the battle of Sekigahara (1600).

GEKOKUJŌ "Those below overthrow those above." A term descriptive of social upheaval, especially during the Muromachi period. Also used to describe the behavior of young, activist military officers in the 1930s.

GENRŌ An extraconstitutional body of elder statesmen of the Meiji period whose primary function was to select Prime Ministers. Saionji Kimmochi, who died in 1940, was the "last of the genrō."

GOKENIN Housemen or direct vassals of the Kamakura Shogun.

HAIKU Poetic form consisting of three lines of five, seven, and five syllables; perfected by Bashō (1644–94).

HAN Territories ruled by daimyos during the Tokugawa period.

HANIWA Terra cotta cylinders and figurines found in burial chambers of the tomb period.

HAMBATSU "Han cliques." Cliques or factions of the Meiji period and later based on *han* origins. The best known were the Satsuma and Chōshū cliques.

JITŌ Stewards. Shogunal housemen of the Kamakura period who were appointed to estates.

KABANE Special titles granted to clan leaders by the imperial court during the pre-Nara age. Originally these titles seem to have designated specific offices or functions, but later they became simply ornaments of prestige for the great clans.

KAIKOKU Policy of the late Tokugawa period. Its advocates called for abandonment of the seclusion laws and "opening of the country" to foreign intercourse.

KAMIKAZE "Divine wind" or "wind of the gods."

KATAKANA, HIRAGANA Syllabic scripts evolved during the Heian period which, in conjunction with Chinese characters, have since been used to write the Japanese language.

KŌAN Themes or problems used in Zen Buddhist practice.

KOKUBUNJI Provincial branch temples constructed during the Nara period.

KOKUTAI A term with strongly chauvinistic overtones which is usually translated as "national polity" or "national essence." To prewar Japanese it implied, among other things, those traditional institutions of Japan, especially the imperial institution, which were seen as unchanging.

KYAKU-SHIKI Supplementary provisions to the *ritsu-ryō* of the Taihō Code.

MIYABI "Courtliness." Used to describe the ideals of beauty, refinement, and perfect forms evolved in Japan's early court tradition.

NEMBUTSU Invocation of the name of Amida Buddha.

NŌ A dramatic art form, centered on a highly stylized type of dance, which was perfected in the fourteenth and fifteenth centuries.

OKASHI "Light" and "witty." A quality found especially in the Heian period miscellany, *Pillow Book*.

RENGA Linked verse, particularly popular during the medieval age (Kamakura and Muromachi periods).

RITSU-RYŌ Penal and administrative provisions of the Taihō Code (701) based on the legal forms of T'ang China.

RŌNIN "Wave people." A term used variously in different periods, but nearly always with the meaning of socially displaced or unclassified people. In the Nara period, for example, *rōnin* meant peasants who had abandoned their fields; in the Tokugawa period it was used to designate masterless samurai.

SABI "Loneliness." Also used as an aesthetic term to express appreciation for that which is aged and withered.

SEITAI Political organs of a particular period, which were considered changeable. Prewar Japanese contrasted this term with *kokutai* (see above).

SHIMPAN DAIMYŌ Daimyos of the Tokugawa period who were branch relatives of the shogunal house.

SHŌEN Estate, manor, or proprietorship.

TOKUSEI Literally, "virtuous administration"; but used as a term for debt-cancellation decrees, which were first issued by the Kamakura Shogunate.

TOZAMA DAIMYŌ Outside daimyos. Daimyos of the Tokugawa period who were neither hereditary vassals to nor relatives of the shogunal house.

UJI Clan; *ujibito*, clan member; *ujigami*, clan deity; *uji no kami*, clan leader.

UKIYO-E Pictures of the "floating world" of the Tokugawa period.

WAKA Classical form of poetry consisting of thirty-one syllables (five lines of five, seven, five, seven, and seven syllables).

WAKŌ "Japanese pirates" of the Muromachi period, but probably included Chinese, Koreans, and others.

YŪGEN An aesthetic term used to describe the profound and the mysterious; associated especially with the *nō* theatre.

ZA Medieval guilds.

ZAIBATSU Great industrial combines.

ZAZEN Sitting in meditation.

GUIDE TO ILLUSTRATIVE MATERIALS

Probably the best single source for illustrative materials on Japan is the Japan Society, 250 Park Avenue, New York, New York 10017. The Society regularly publishes information on available films, display photographs, exhibit materials, traveling exhibitions, etc. dealing with Japan. It also has its own library of 16mm sound films which may be borrowed by members of the Society.

The Asia Society, 112 East 64th Street, New York, New York 10021, is another good source for general information on illustrative materials.

A limited number of critically acclaimed Japanese feature films, including *Rashōmon, Gate of Hell,* and *Ugetsu,* are available from Cinema Guild, Inc., 10 Fiske Place, Mt. Vernon, New York 10550 (or Audio Film Center, 522 Clement Street, San Francisco, California 94118 or 2138 East 75th Street, Chicago, Illinois 60649). Other 16mm sound films on the crafts, customs, industries, sights, etc. of Japan may be obtained from Ideal Pictures, Inc., which has three locations:

321 West 44th Street, New York, New York 10036
417 North State Street, Chicago, Illinois 60610
1840 Alcatraz Avenue, Berkeley, California 94703

The Japan National Tourist Organization, 45 Rockefeller Plaza, New York, New York 10020, makes available on free loan a number of 16mm sound and color films for group showings at colleges and before clubs and other organizations.

Maps of Japan may, of course, be obtained from most regular dealers. Denoyer-Geppert Co., 5235 Ravenwood Avenue, Chicago, Illinois 60640, seems to have an unusually wide selection of physical, political, visual relief, land use, etc. maps of Japan In addition, it has a number of sectional or regional maps which show Japan in relation to the other countries of East Asia and the Pacific.

PB-11271
5-23

RENEWALS 691-4574

DATE DUE